STAGES

Literature of Newfoundland and Labrador

Book 2

edited by

Eric Norman
June Warr
Ray Goulding

BREAKWATER

Canada's Atlantic Publisher

Cover photograph: "A Fish Stage in Pouch Cove", taken by **Michael Messner** *of M.J.M. Photographics.*

Canadian Cataloguing in Publication Data

Main entry under title:

Stages

(Literature of Newfoundland and Labrador ; book 2)

For use in Grade 8

ISBN 978-0-919948-92-1

1. Canadian literature (English) — Newfoundland.*
2. Canadian literature (English) — Labrador.*
I. Norman, Eric. II. Warr, June. III. Goulding, Ray. IV. Series.

PS8255.N4P38 C810'.8'09718 C80-094850-5
PR9198.2.N42P38

Reprinted in 1997, 2001 and 2007

TO THE TEACHER

This book is one in a series of Newfoundland literature anthologies designed for junior high school use. The need for such a series has long been felt by teachers of English in the province, and has been recognized by the Department of Education in its objectives for the English program.

Each book is arranged thematically, with some attempt to arrange works chronologically within each theme. Four major themes appear in each text. These deal with the way of life of our forebears in this country; the physical surroundings and environment in which we live; the values, attitudes and discriminations which we might see around us or experience; and the sense of community, of caring for our province, which is so much a part of our people. Minor themes appear at intervals in the three books, to bring to the attention of students our writers' treatment of other aspects of our country and people, such as our sense of humour; the place held by our province's original inhabitants; the tremendously varied and rich flora and fauna of our land; and the heroes and heroines of our people.

Our authors are drawn from the whole spectrum of Newfoundland writing, spanning geography and time. Many writers appearing in these texts have not previously been published other than in magazines or periodicals. Others are well-known and prolific. Some are polished professionals, some are talented amateurs, while others write directly and simply from the heart of experience. They all have something of value for our young people.

The format of the work is straightforward, and should help teachers present the material positively to the students. Each theme unit has a brief introduction which illuminates the aspects of the theme to be treated. Each selection within the theme has a background introduction which usually highlights as well some literary concept to be noticed in the piece. At the end of each piece is a brief biography of the author (unless the biography had appeared in an earlier selection), questions and activities which will develop further understanding of the selection, and suggestions which will help relate the literature class to other activities within the school.

Throughout the books words which may cause trouble are marked * and appear in a simple glossary at the back.

The editors suggest that classes engaged in enjoying this series should have access to at least a good wall map of the province, a library selection which includes at least the titles referred to in the series, and suitable audio-visual material available from the Department of Education, especially the series entitled "Communication Newfoundland Style." Subscriptions to Newfoundland magazines and periodicals, use of television and radio programmes with Newfoundland content, involvement in local productions by drama groups, and arranged visits to the school by local authors are all avenues which should be explored as the opportunities arise.

Each text may be treated as a unit within the regular English program, or its content may be used selectively by the teacher in an integrated approach. It is suggested, though, that material not cross over grade lines as this may lead to boredom or frustration for the student.

In choosing the selections for these texts the editors were very much aware of the reading levels and interests of the audience for which they were intended. This automatically eliminated a large part of our literature, especially that written more than fifty years ago, and practically all scholarly works. Unfortunately these factors and the restricted size of the texts also eliminated most of our drama and one or two of our major writers.

Considerable difficulty and frustration was experienced in locating literature to adequately represent Labrador. The trouble lay not so much in locating literature of Labrador as in locating writings that would be meaningful and of interest to junior high school students, and which also were written at a comprehension and vocabulary level suitable for junior high students. This proved to be a very difficult problem considering that one of our intentions in developing the series at the junior high level was to expose students in a positive way to their own literature so that enjoyment is enhanced and liking for the literature established. It is intended that more scholarly and literary approaches should be left to the high school grades. This meant that although a search was conscientiously made, Labrador literature is still not as well represented in the series as we would have liked. The same problem was encountered in this junior high series in finding suitable literature representing native peoples, ethnic groups and early chronological periods. It is our hope that these shortcomings will be corrected in material for the senior high school grades where the maturity of the student will give greater range to selection criteria.

Throughout the compilation of the series the editors were guided generally by Department guidelines and the desired outcomes which were established initially by the editorial group. It was felt that students who work positively through the series will have a good knowledge of, and pride in, their heritage, and will be readily able to see why a person with a background in this province will often have a unique point of view when dealing with issues and concerns which may be universal. They will realize that Newfoundland literature is real and legitimate literature, thinking of it in the context of literature in the English-speaking world, and they will have a good knowledge of the works and background biographies of major writers in this province, and will know something of their styles. Our students will be more alert to and appreciative of the various possibilities for take-off points for writing and acting, or for expressing themselves through the other art forms, such as painting, sketching, song or music. They will also be aware that Newfoundland literature exists in a multitude of forms, from the oral literature of folksongs to the polished work of modern writers. They will also begin to understand that dialects and patterns of speech coming to us from the past, far from being inferior things of shame, are unique and valuable in their own right, and are legitimate subjects for further study.

The series was prepared by teachers, aware that an essential ingredient for its success is the teaching which will be applied to it. We have been accustomed to thinking of the books as ours; but they are now yours as well, and we wish you much joy as you engage your students in their use.

E.N.
J.W.
R.G.

Contents

Peter Ball

Ben Hansen

FOREBEARS

Part One

We Are A Family

Most of the selections in this unit are about families in the past. When our parents and grandparents spoke of their families it was with a feeling of closeness, a suggestion of all for one, one for all. This dependency on each other was determined more by necessity than by choice. They earned their livelihood through hard work on the sea and land, and that often required many "hands" working with each other to provide just enough food or money to allow some security all year round.

Families were large in those days, ten children was common, and often this family lived in the same house with grandparents and grandchildren. So everybody lived together and "all hands pitched in" to get the work finished.

To contrast with the circumstances of days gone by we have included a brief scene from a modern family. You will perhaps be surprised at the great differences suggested.

Being a part of a family, then or now, means more than work, and if you listen closely to the voices of Ted Russell, Elizabeth Goudie, Florence Barbour, Norman Duncan and Helen Porter you will come to appreciate what that "more" is. As you read think about how families are different today.

Getting Ready To Read

Being a member of a family brings many responsibilities, but one major responsibility of every member is to help take care of every other member.

But one member of a family always needs more help and attention than any other. That person is, of course, the baby. There are times when parents have to leave the house, and must leave the caring for the baby in the hands of someone else. This someone else may be an older brother or sister, and sometimes it's a grandparent. In the selection "Babysittin' " the member of the family left to babysit is Grampa Walcott, assisted by a bachelor, Uncle Mose Mitchell. Their experience with Grampa's grandson is not one that can be easily forgotten.

Babysittin'

Of all the jobs I've ever done in this world, the one I never want to do agen is babysittin'. Yes, I had a good dory-mate, Grampa Walcott, and we come through safe and sound, but when I think of it — never agen!

Grampa was stuck that night, good and proper. Grandma and her daughter Aunt Sophy, and her daughter Soos, who was visitin' from Corner Brook with her six-months' old baby, had all been out to this special party the Women's Association was givin' — on account of three generations of members bein' here all at the one time.

Of course, they could've got Liz Noddy, Jethro's daughter, to babysit, but she would have chewed bubble gum all night, and brought along her grammy-phone records (the ones Grampa can't stand). He said a night like that would've drove him cracked. So that evenin', he asked me if I'd take a berth with him babysittin', and I signed on. Well, from now on, whatever babysittin' there is in Pigeon Inlet, can be done by Liz Noddy, with her bubble gum, All Shook Up, Jailhouse Rock and all the rest of it.

The women had gone when I got there. The baby was sound asleep upstairs and Grampa had the cribbage board all set up on the kitchen table. I asked him did he have any instructions what to do if the baby woke. He said no, Soos had made some funny remark about a formula* bein' somewhere, but bein' as how the only formula he knew about was the one for findin' the number of cords in a pile of pulp wood, we figured that had no connection with the baby. So we started our game of cribbage.

The women had said they'd be home before ten, but bein' women, there was no sign of 'em at half-past, when the baby started to bawl. We waited to see if the squall'd die down, but it got so bad 'twas likely to frighten all the neighbours, so Grampa went up and brought him down.

When that baby grows up, it won't cost him much in soap to wash his face. All he'd have to do is open his mouth and there'll be no face left to wash. Grampa had him wrong end up when he brought him down but even after he upended him right, he bawled harder than ever. I made signs to Grampa (there was no sense tryin' to talk), that there must be a pin stickin' in him somewhere. Grampa held him up sort of by the crosstrees, while I examined among his riggin'. Next thing I knew, the whole outfit tumbled to the kitchen floor, and there he was in his bare poles, bawlin', if 'twas possible, harder than ever.

Grampa screeched out something to me about gettin' the canvas back on him quick, but like I told him, anybody with one eye or for that matter, nar eye at all, could tell we weren't supposed to put that back on him. We agreed that the only thing to do was poke it into the kitchen stove and look in the sail locker for a new outfit. We located the sail locker on top of the sewin' machine and after an argument as to whether we should put a jib on him or a foresail, we put both of 'em on. Like Grampa said, 'twas best to play safe. The trouble was it only made him bawl more than ever. "There's only one salvation," said Grampa. "Grub. 'Twould have been better," said he, "if Soos had told us what to feed him instead of talkin' about cords of pulpwood."

But what could we feed a young fellow that age? There was cold moose meat in the pantry, but, like Grampa said, the rough edges might choke him. Something smooth we wanted, but what? There was only one thing — made to order, you might say. Fat pork. So I took him, while Grampa headed for the pork barrel in the backroom and come back with a lovely little chunk, 'bout a half inch each way.

But I had misgivin's. There was no question as to smoothness, or even nourishment. But with no teeth to chew it, supposin' it gave him indigestion. Grampa had the answer to that. Tie a string to it. Then after he'd gone to sleep on it, if it hurt him, we had the wherewithal to get it back.

And that's what we did. He swallered that hunk of salt pork like a real north-shoreman, and before Grampa had him halfway up the stairs he was half asleep, and quiet as a mouse.

'Twas then this horrible thought struck me. Supposin' he swallowed the string too. But when Grampa got downstairs he said as how he'd thought of that very danger, and had belayed the other end of the string to the baby's big toe. "But," said I, "when you laid him down didn't he stick up his legs and slacken the string?" "Yes," said Grampa, "he did, and then I tied a sheepshank* on it to tighten it again. Then when he dozes off and straightens his legs, up 'twill come, easy as anything."

Five minutes later by Grampa's clock, he creeped up again, and there was the youngster, sound asleep, with his legs straightened out. Grampa untied the string from his toe, picked up the other end off the pillow, and we had both that string and the fat pork in the kitchen stove on top of that other thing, just as we heard the women comin' back from the party.

First thing Soos did after we remarked on how quiet the baby was, was to go to the warmin' oven and take out what she called the "formula." And when I saw what it was, I got out of there quick, because the next thing she might do would be to overhaul the contents of the sail locker.

Perhaps, like I told Grampa next day, we shouldn't have burnt that thing, but Grampa said "nonsense! Soos got so many of 'em she'd never miss one." Besides, what else in the world could we have done with it?

Ted Russell

In the 1950s Edward Russell was known to many Newfoundlanders as Uncle Mose. Every week Uncle Mose was heard on CBC Radio's Fisheries Broadcast telling stories about characters and events in the imaginary outport of Pigeon Inlet. In these stories Russell tried to show the values possessed by ordinary Newfoundlanders whom he had come to know and respect through thirty years of working among them as a teacher and magistrate. During his career he worked in Millertown, Pass Island, Harbour Breton, Channel, Fogo and St. John's. He spent two years in the first cabinet formed by Premier Smallwood in 1949, but resigned on a point of principle. In addition to his Fisheries broadcast scripts, some of which have been published as **The Chronicles of Uncle Mose** *and* **Tales From Pigeon Inlet,** *Ted Russell wrote two plays:* **The Holdin' Ground** *and* **The Hangashore.** *Mr. Russell was born in 1904 and died in 1977.*

Understanding What You Have Read

1. Explain why Grampa Walcott and Uncle Mose agreed to babysit.

2. What relation was the baby to Grampa Walcott?

3. a) What is meant by "formula", as it is used by Soos?
   b) How does Grampa's misunderstanding of the meaning of "formula" cause him a problem?
   c) How did Grampa solve the problem?

4. What qualities did salt pork have as a suitable food for the baby? What was its danger? How was the danger removed?

Things To Do

1. It is obvious from his choice of words and phrases that the speaker, Uncle Mose, is a fisherman — sailor. In the first paragraph he calls his babysittin' partner "a good dory-mate." Find other seaman's words and phrases used by the speaker.

2. A technique or device used by Ted Russell to create humour is exaggeration. That is, he blows up or stretches the truth so the humour in the situation will be clearer and funnier. For example, Uncle Mose exaggerates when he says the baby's bawlin' "got so bad 'twas likely to frighten all the neighbours." What are several other examples of exaggeration in "Babysittin' "?

3. Write a paragraph in which you tell a story that makes use of exaggeration.

* * *

David Wegenast / DECK'S AWASH

Getting Ready To Read

"Baby Bruce" is only a small selection from Elizabeth Goudie's autobiography called *Woman of Labrador*. You will notice very quickly the simple language the writer uses. She writes simply because she had only four years of formal schooling. She had no further education other than that which her life's experience gave her. The writings of such people as Mrs. Goudie we describe as folk literature. Folk literature usually is written on a very simple level, using a narrow vocabulary and short simple sentences. However, it is often filled with emotion and wisdom, experience and love, which make it enjoyable and good and valuable.

When the accident described in "Baby Bruce" happened, Mrs. Goudie was twenty-five years old, and living in a cabin on the coast of Labrador with her husband Jim and her four children. It was 1927.

Baby Bruce

October passed by and Jim went setting his traps again. The first evening he was gone I was alone cleaning my floor. I looked around for my children. The girl Marie and the second boy Bruce were sitting by the stove watching the fire burning. I checked them to see if everything was all right and went on about my work. About ten minutes later, the whole house lit up with fire. I jumped to my feet and I was by Bruce's side in a minute. I did not know what to do; I saw a big coat close by and caught it and smothered out the flame. For a few seconds, he didn't move. I picked him up and the minute I moved him he went into a "rock of pain." I was a whole hour trying to keep him on my lap. That was between five and six in the evening; at about six-thirty, he fell asleep. Jim was still not home so I laid Bruce on a big wooden chest I had beside the table. I thought I would have something to eat because I expected to be up all night. I looked over his body as carefully as I could and I saw his right arm was burnt right to his body, and one cheek, one ear and both his lips were burned, so I knew I had a terrible task on my hands. I tried to eat but couldn't. I walked the floor and the other children were afraid that their little brother would die and they were crying. Their daddy was not home yet.

About seven o'clock I heard the boat coming and I was there with my little boy all burnt. I did not know how his dad would take it. I thought that he might think that I had been careless and got him burnt so I just sat by my little boy and waited for Jim to come into the house. I told him what had happened. We sat beside our child and when he woke up he again went into a rock of pain. We walked the floor with him the whole night taking turns.

He could not even take a drink during the whole night. In the morning, he seemed to be better and asked for a drink. Then he fell asleep so we had a chance to look over his whole body. There were burns on his legs as well as his arm and face. We sat down and tried to figure out what we could do. The only thing we had in the house was a bottle of castor oil. I said to Jim, "You better get me a juniper stick and I will boil it and use the liquid to bathe the burns." I had no dressing. I had a couple of sheets and I tore them up for dressings. There was a small wound of open flesh on his elbow and I was really afraid that would become infected. I hoped and prayed it would be all right. Jim got the juniper stick. I went to work and boiled it four hours and started to bathe the wounds in the liquid.

On the second day, the spot of his elbow looked a bit red and infected. I took a piece of the stick and peeled the outside bark off and took the inside, the gummy bark of the stick, and beat it to a pulp. I sterilized my dressing by browning it on the stove and I placed a piece of the gummy pulp on his elbow. I greased the poultice* with the castor oil and after six days he seemed to be getting a lot better.

There was a doctor at Nain with an explorer, Captain MacMillan from the United States. They were stationed at Nain but traveled all the time. MacMillan's doctor traveled to Hopedale and used to travel north to Okak, so we didn't know if he was in Nain or not. After eight days, my husband thought our little boy was better. Jim went out to Davis Inlet and waited for a day. On the second day, the doctor passed through Davis Inlet on his way to Nain.

Jim brought him up the bay the next morning. He looked at our boy and at what I was using and he said he was over the worst. He told me to carry on with what I was using. He gave me some dressings and I was very happy about what he told me. He said I had done a marvellous job so my mind was at ease then.

I was still sick myself from the infant fever and I had lost a lot of weight. The doctor said to me, "You should be in a hospital yourself." I was so frightened when the baby was burned that I hadn't eaten for four or five days. Jim stayed home with me for a month. It was three weeks before I could dress my little boy. I had three other children and the youngest was only two months old. We both worked night and day for about three weeks. With hard work we helped to save our little boy. We were both upset for a week because we did not know what was going to happen. You can't imagine what we went through that fall but the main thing is that we got through and our little boy got well again. Many, many times after, we both wondered how we had done it. But with God's help, we fought for his life together. For three weeks neither of us had a full night's sleep but the main thing was that he lived and we were both very thankful. When two people work so hard together to try to save a child, it is good to see him recover.

Elizabeth Goudie

As a Labrador woman Elizabeth Goudie hunted, fished, made clothing, raised vegetables, suffered cold, isolation and the threat of wild animals. She raised eight children and fought against disease and death in her family. Her outstanding qualities of strength, sense of proportion and her sense of humour are displayed for readers in her book **Woman of Labrador,** *which she began writing for her children and grand children. She is today perhaps the best-known Labradorian in Canada. Memorial University has recognized her contribution to Newfoundland life by awarding her an honorary doctorate. Mrs. Goudie lives in Happy Valley and is presently working on a second book.*

Understanding What You Have Read

1. What happened for Baby Bruce to be burned? Was he badly burned?

2. What do you think a "rock of pain" is?

3. How did Mrs. Goudie and her husband spend the first night with Baby Bruce?

4. a) Why didn't Mrs. Goudie take Baby Bruce to a doctor?
   b) How did she treat Baby Bruce's burns?
   c) Was she a good nurse?

5. a) How long did it take Baby Bruce to recover?
   b) Why, according to Mrs. Goudie, were they able to save her baby's life?

Things To Do

1. To better appreciate what Mrs. Goudie had to do imagine what your parent would do if you were very badly burned. Write a description of the actions he or she would take from the moment he or she discovered you were burned until you were safely recovering.

2. Borrow from the library *Woman of Labrador* by Elizabeth Goudie and read this very interesting story.

* * *

Getting Ready To Read

This selection is from a book by Florence Barbour entitled *Memories of Life on the Labrador and in Newfoundland.* The author explains as she narrates so that the reader is taken back in time to share her experiences, we call this type of writing autobiography.

Notice how these people changed work into an outing or pleasure trip. There is probably a lesson to be learned here that when we enjoy our work it becomes much more rewarding and pleasurable.

Bradeau for Bake-Apples

When August came, we always looked forward to a trip up Bradeau Bay for bake-apples. In size and flavor the Labrador bake-apple excels that of Newfoundland. Hundreds of gallons, not cooked, but with water added, would be put into barrels, brought home, and shared with less fortunate neighbors. Mother always made jam in plentiful supply, not only for our own use and for giving away to friends, but several dozen jars made especially for R.B. Job, who was my father's boss. We also put the ripe berries without water into bottles of all descriptions, which, when carefully corked and covered with hot pitch, were air-tight and preserved the berries indefinitely. These berries formed their own juice and when served with cream, they made a most delicious dessert. There were no preserving jars in those days, or deep freezers, so one had to use a little ingenuity* instead. I guess if any Newfoundlanders outside the country read this story, their mouths will be watering like mine and their tongues will be hanging out for some of those bake-apples and cream right now. Yum, yum!

The trip to Bradeau for bake-apples was considered a privilege. None of us would miss it unless sickness laid us low. Due preparations were made the night before, if father considered the weather suitable. Early in the morning when we were all 'torights' (Newfoundland expression meaning "ready"), we started out in one of the largest motor boats. We were well-supplied with cooking utensils, such as a frying pan, iron bake pot, large saucepan, and a kettle, of course. A two-

and-a-half gallon galvanized* water bucket and a mug was part of everyone's equipment, and a bottle of Citronella oil to combat the mosquitoes. There was also the rounder* or leggy, which Newfoundlanders nearly always carry on a picnic. After being soaked overnight, the rounder was wrapped in wet paper, thrown on the fire, and allowed to stay there until it was cooked. Nothing tastes quite like it out in the country, where one's appetite is always keen.

When we arrived we immediately "boiled up", as most people say. We had had a hurried breakfast, and a long ride in the open boat, and the fresh air made us hungry. A fireplace of rocks was quickly built on the beach where we also found a long stick on which to sling the kettle over the fire, and plenty of dry kindling, which most Newfoundlanders call "crunnicks". Quite often we would find a blasty* bough to help get the fire really going. After our mug-up everyone was left to fadge* for himself and seek out a good marsh for the berries. One of us girls would be the self-appointed cook and washer-up for the day, and would pick the berries nearby to make jam to cook some doughboys*. When dinner time came, the cook would stand on a boulder or high ridge, and send out a loud, long, and lusty call. The dinner usually consisted of tinned rabbit and onions, with gravy and potatoes, followed by doughboys in hot jam. The feast was fit for a king, and the mugs of tea might have been a nectar* for the gods.

After the meal, everyone was reluctant to leave the smokey atmosphere of the fireplace. But to go home without our buckets full of berries was unthinkable, so off everyone trudged again. Sometimes the cook went along as well and helped whoever was picking near the fireplace. Our code of honor was that if one person had his bucket full, he or she would automatically begin to help out someone less lucky. Gradually the pickers wandered back to the fireplace and the kettle was put on once more. After being in the marshes where the mosquitoes were quite thick, it was good to get back to the water's edge. Sometimes we purposely made a fire to create a smoke by putting some blackberry bushes and moss on the lighted embers*. Sitting in the lea* of this we quickly got rid of any flies which had decided to make their home in one's hair or down one's neck. The second meal was usually fresh cod if we were lucky enough to jig one on the way along, or the salted leggy, followed by some pork toutens* or bangbelly* made the night before.

Having loaded our buckets and satisfied the inner man, we started on our trip home. Sometimes the sea would be as calm as a mill pond, at other times it might be stormy and treacherous. If a southwest breeze sprang up just as the tide turned in the opposite direction, getting out of Bradeau Bay and around Long Point would require a feat of good seamanship. One such trip I remember was really dangerous. Knowing that Hubert was at the helm and in charge, however, gave us all the assurance that all would be well. He proved himself that day to be one of the best. There were times when he almost gave the order for the men to dump the buckets of berries. Seven galvanized buckets full of berries dumped overboard would definitely have helped to lighten the boat and thus prevent our being swamped by the heavy seas. Our parents were watching from Isle-au-Bois and told us afterwards that they were very anxious for our safety. At times we would sink down into those blue-green mountains of sea so far that all we could see was water, and our parents would lose sight of us; then up again we would come to plunge full blast into the breaking top of another huge Atlantic roller. Each time we went down our parents thought for sure we would be swamped, but, no, up again and again we came, until we reached the calmer water near Isle-au-Bois, and every one gave a sigh of relief. I can well imagine our parents said a prayer of thankfulness that day because four of the family had been in the boat.

When we reached home, whether we were "tuckered out," "fair wore out," or just plain tired and weary, we always delayed just long enough to display our berries, wash up, and bathe our fly bites with vinegar and water; then, although it may have seemed early, we were glad to go to bed. The trip had given us a sense of exhilaration and well-being, which came from the long ride in the open boat, the long trek* over the marshes, a full load of berries, and the thrilling, though dangerous, ride home. How good it was to feel the cool linen sheets, and I for one hardly knew when "the pillow struck my head."

Florence Barbour

Florence Barbour was born and lived at Blanc Sablon in Labrador. She has published **Memories of Life on the Labrador and in Newfoundland**

Understanding What You Have Read

1. In this piece of writing what do the following words mean?

   hot pitch
   rounder or leggy
   crunnicks
   blasty bough
   fadge
   pork toutens
   bangbelly

2. The author shows the fickleness of nature. Give an example from the selection which shows that nature can be with you one minute and against you the next.

3. Do you and your family or friends do anything today which might be termed work, but is, in fact, quite enjoyable? Describe it.

Things To Do

1. Read about some more of Florence Barbour's memories by locating her book in the library.

2. Tell your classmates about a berry-picking or similar trip you have taken.

* * *

Getting Ready To Read

This is one of many stories about Billy Topsail, a young Newfoundland boy who lived in an outport during the early part of this century. The story is fiction, of course, but much of the substance, (such as the language, the materials and the relationships between the men and the boy), is typical of the time. Norman Duncan lived on the Canadian mainland, but spent many summers in small Newfoundland outports, enjoying the life and coming to love the people.

Notice as you read this story the emphasis which is placed on obedience, loyalty, patience, strength and endurance. These are all qualities which Duncan saw and admired in the people of the outports.

Billy Topsail

I

Billy Goes Seal Hunting

What befell old Tom Topsail and his crew came in the course of the day's work. Fishermen and seal hunters, such as the folk of Ruddy Cove, may not wait for favorable weather: when the fish are running, they must fish; when the seals are on the drift-ice* in the spring, they must hunt.

So on that day when the seals were sighted by the watch on Lookout Head, it was a matter of course that the men of the place should set out to the hunt.

Bill Watt, his mate, scanned the sky in the northeast. It was heavy, cold, and leaden* — fluffy grey towards the zenith*, and black where the clouds met the barren hills.

"I s'pose," he said, " that 'twill blow, too."

"Oh, aye," Topsail replied indifferently, "snow 'n' blow. We'll know what 'twill do when it begins," he added. "Billy, b'y!" he shouted.

In response Billy Topsail came bounding down the rocky path from the cottage. He was stout for his age, with broad shoulders, long thick arms, and large hands. There was a boy's flush of expectation on his face, and the flash of a boy's delight in his eyes. He was willing for adventure.

"Bill an' me'll take the rodney*," Topsail drawled. "I s'pose you might's well fetch the punt, an' we'll send you back with the first haul."

"Hooray!" cried Billy; and with that he waved his cap and sped back up the hill.

"Fetch your gaff, lad!" Topsail called after him. "Make haste! There's Joshua Rideout with his sail up. 'Tis time we was off."

"Looks more'n ever like snow," Bill Watt observed while they waited. "I'm thinkin' 'twill snow."

The wind was light, the sea quiet, the sky thinly overcast. Had it not been for the threat of heavy weather in the northeast, it would have been an ideal day for the hunt. The punt and the rodney, the latter far in the lead, ran quietly out from the harbor with their little sails all spread. From the punt Billy Topsail could soon see the small scattered packs of seals — black dots against the white of the ice.

When the rodney made the field, the punts of the harbour fleet had disappeared in the winding lanes of open water that led through the floe.* Tom Topsail was late. The nearer seals were all marked by the hunters who had already landed. The rodney would have to be taken farther in than the most venturesome hunter had yet dared to go — perilously far into the midst of the shifting ice.

"We got to go right in, Bill," said Topsail, as he furled the rodney's sails.

"I s'pose," was Watt's reply, with a backward glance to the northeast. "An' Billy?"

" 'Tis not wise to take him in," Topsail answered hastily. "We'll have him bide here."

II

Billy Is Told To Wait

Billy was hailed and, to his great disappointment, warned to keep beyond the edge of the floe. Then the rodney shot into the lane, with Topsail and Bill Watt rowing like mad. She was soon lost to sight. Billy shipped his sail and paddled to the edge of the ice, to wait, as patiently as might be, for the reappearance of the rodney.

At last there came an ominous* puff of wind. It swept over the sea from the coast, whipping up little waves in its course — frothy little waves that hissed. Heavy flakes of snow began to fall. As the wind rose, they fell faster, and came driving, swirling with it.

With the fall of the first flakes the harbor fleet came pell-mell* from the floe. Not a man among them but wished himself in a sheltered place. Sails were raised in haste, warnings were shouted; then off went the boats, beating up harbor with all sails set.

"Make sail, lad!" old Elisha Bull shouted to Billy, as his punt swung past.

Billy shook his head, "I'll beat back with father!" he cried.

"You'll lose yourself!" Elisha screamed, as a last warning, before his punt carried him out of hail.

But Billy still hung at the edge of the ice. His father had said, "Bide here till we come out," and "bide" there he would.

He kept watch for the rodney, but no rodney came. Minute after minute passed. He hesitated. Was it not his duty to beat home? There was still the chance that he might be able to make the harbor. Did he not owe a duty to his mother — to himself?

But a crashing noise from the floe brought him instantly to a decision. He knew what that noise meant. The ice was feeling the force of the wind. It would pack and move out to sea. The lane by which the rodney had entered then slowly closed.

At once the lad's duty was plain to him. He must stay where he was. If his father and Bill Watt managed to get to the edge of the ice afoot, who else was to take them off?

III

Billy, The Hero Of The Ice Pack

The ice was moving out to sea, Billy knew. The pans were crunching, grinding ever more noisily. But he let the punt drift as near as he dared, and so followed the pack towards the open, keeping watch, ever more hopelessly, for the black forms of the two men.

Soon, so fast did the sea rise, so wild was the wind, his own danger was very great. The ice was like a rocky shore leeward.* He began to fear that he would be wrecked.

Time and again the punt was nearly swamped, but Billy dared not drop the oars to bail. There was something more. His arms, stout and seasoned though they were, were giving out. It would not long be possible to keep the boat off the ice.

At last he came to a cove. It narrowed to a long, winding arm* which apparently extended some distance into the floe. There he found quiet water. He landed without difficulty at a point where the arm was no more than a few yards wide. Dusk was then approaching. The wind was bitterly cold, and the snow was thick and blinding.

It would not be safe, he knew, to leave the boat in the water, for at any moment the shifting pans might close and crush it. He tried to lift it out of the water, but his strength was not sufficient. He managed to get the bow on the ice; that was all.

"I'll just have to leave it," he thought. "I'll just have to trust that 'twill not be nipped."

Near by there was a hummock* of ice. He sought the lee of it, and there, protected from the wind, he sat down to wait.

Often, when the men were spinning yarns in the cottages of Ruddy Cove of a winter night, he had listened, open-mouthed, to the tales of seal hunters who had been cast away. Now he was himself drifting out to sea. He had no fire, no food, no shelter but a hummock of ice. He had the bitterness of the night to pass through — the hunger of tomorrow to face.

"But sure," he muttered with characteristic hopefulness, "I've a boat, an' many a man has been cast away without one."

He thought he had better make another effort to haul the boat on the ice. Some movement of the pack might close the arm where it floated. So he stumbled toward the place.

He stared round in amazement and alarm; then he uttered a cry of terror. The open water had disappeared.

"She's been nipped!" he sobbed. "She's been nipped — nipped to splinters! I've lost meself!"

Night came fast. An hour before, so dense was the storm,

nothing had been visible sixty paces away; now nothing was to be seen anywhere. Where was the rodney? Had his father and Bill Watt escaped from the floe by some new opening? Were they safe at home? Were they still on the floe? He called their names. The swish of the storm, the cracking and crunching of the ice as the wind swept it on — that was all that he heard.

For a long time he sat in dull despair. He hoped no longer.

By and by, when it was deep night, something occurred to distract him. He caught sight of a crimson glow, flaring and fading. It seemed to be in the sky, now far off, now near at hand. He started up.

"What's that?" he muttered.

IV

What Happened to Tom and Bill?

Meanwhile, under the powerful strokes of old Tom Topsail and Bill Watt, the rodney had followed the open leads into the heart of the floe. From time to time Watt muttered a warning; but the spirit of the hunt fully possessed Tom, and his only cry was: "Push on! Push on!"

Seal after seal escaped, while the sky darkened. He was only the more determined not to go back empty-handed.

"I tells you," Watt objected, "we'll not get out. There's the wind now. And snow, man — snow!"

Topsail thought no more about seals. The storm was fairly upon them. His only concern was to escape from the floe. He was glad, indeed, that Billy had not followed them. He had that, at least, to be thankful for.

They turned the boat. Bending to the oars, they followed the lane by which they had entered. Confusion came with the wind and snow.

"Trapped!" muttered Watt.

"Aye, lad," Topsail said solemnly, "trapped!"

They rested on their oars. Ice was on every hand. They stared into each other's eyes.

Then for the second time Watt ran his glance over the shores of the lake in which they floated. He started, then pointed in the direction from which they had come. Topsail needed no word of explanation. The ice was closing in. The pressure of the pack beyond would soon obliterate* the lake. They rowed desperately for the nearest shore.

When the boat struck the ice Watt jumped ashore with the painter*. Topsail, leaping from seat to seat, followed instantly. At that moment there was a loud crack like a clap of thunder. It was followed by a crunching noise.

"It's comin'!" screamed Topsail.

"Heave away!"

They caught the bow, lifted it out of the water, and with a unified effort slowly hauled it out of harm's way. A moment later there was no sign of open water.

"Thank God!" gasped Topsail.

Now they sat silent in the lee of the upturned boat, with the snow swirling about them; again they ran madly back and forth; yet again they swung their arms and stamped their feet. At last, do what they would, they shivered all the time. Then they sat quietly down.

"I'm wonderful glad Billy is safe home," Watt observed.

"I wisht I was sure o' that," said Topsail. "It looks bad for us, Bill, lad. The ice is drivin' out fast, an' I'm thinkin' 'twill blow steady for a day. It looks wonderful bad for us, an' I'd feel — easier in me mind — about the lad's mother — if I knowed he was safe home."

Late in the night Topsail turned to Watt. He had to nudge him to get his attention. "It's awful cold, Bill," he said. "We got the boat, lad. Eh? We got the boat."

"No, no, Tom! Not yet! We'd be sure doomed without the boat."

Half an hour passed. Again Topsail roused Watt.

"We're doomed if we don't," he said. "We can't stand it till mornin', lad. We can't wait no longer."

Watt blundered to his feet. Without a word he fumbled in the snow until he found what he sought. It was the axe. He handed it to Topsail.

"Do it, Tom!" he said thickly. "I'm near gone."

Topsail attacked the boat. It was like murder, he thought. He struck blow after blow, blindly, viciously; gathered the splinters, made a little heap of them, and set them afire. The fire blazed brightly. Soon it was roaring. The ice all around was lighted up. Above, the snow reflected the lurid* glow.

Warmth and a cheerful light put life in the men. They crept as close to the fire as they could. Reason would shut out hope altogether, but hope came to them. Might not the storm abate? Might not the wind change? Might not they be picked up? In this strain they talked for a long time; and meanwhile they added the fuel, splinter by splinter!

V

When Morning Came

"Father! 'Tis you!"

Topsail leaped to his feet and stared.

" 'Tis Billy!" cried Watt.

Billy staggered into the circle of light. He stared stupidly at the fire. Then he tottered a step or two nearer and stood swaying, and again he stared at the fire in a stupid way.

"I seed the fire!" he mumbled. "The punt's nipped, sir — an' I seed the fire — an' crawled over the ice. 'Twas hard to find you."

Tom Topsail and Bill Watt understood. They, too, had travelled rough ice in a blizzard, and they understood.

Billy was wet to the waist. That meant that blinded by the snow or deceived by the night, he had slipped through some opening in the ice, some crack or hole. The bare thought of that lonely peril* was enough to make the older men shudder. But they asked him no questions. They led him to the fire, and set him down between them. By and by he was so far recovered that he was able to support his father's argument that the wind had not changed.

"Oh, well," replied Watt, doggedly, "you can say what you likes, but I tells you that the wind's veered to the south. 'Twould not surprise me if the pack was drivin' Cape Wonder way."

"No, no, Bill," said Topsail, sadly, "there's been no change. We're drivin' straight out. When the wind drops the pack'll go to pieces, an' then — "

They argued until near dawn. Of a sudden they heard a low, far-off rumble. It was a terrifying noise. It ran toward them. It was like the bumping that runs through a freight-train when the engine comes to a sudden stop.

The pack trembled. There was then a fearful confusion of grinding, crashing sounds. Everywhere the ice was heaving and turning. The smaller pans were crushed; many of the greater ones were forced on end; some were lifted bodily out of the water, and fell back in fragments, broken by their own weight. On all sides were noise and awful upheaval. The great pan upon which the seal hunters had landed was tipped up-up-up — until it was like the side of a steep hill. There it rested. Then came silence.

Bill Watt was right; the wind had changed; the pack had grounded on Cape Wonder. The three men from Ruddy Cove walked ashore in the morning.

Norman Duncan

Norman Duncan (1871-1916) was born in Brantford, Ontario. During the summer of 1900 he visited the Exploits area of Notre Dame Bay and quickly became entranced by the environment and the people he found there. For five or more consecutive years he returned to Newfoundland to spend his summers, delighting in his surroundings and coming to respect and admire the people he lived among. These summer experiences provided the material and inspiration for his numerous short stories, essays and novels set in Newfoundland. He published **The Way of the Sea** *(1903),* **Dr. Luke of the Labrador** *(1904),* **Dr. Grenfell's Parish** *(1905) and* **The Cruise of The Shining Light** *(1907). He is best known by younger readers for his two collections of short stories* **The Adventures of Billy Topsail** *and* **Billy Topsail and Company.**

Understanding What You Have Read

1. Billy and the others use words which are not in use as much today, such as "seed" for "saw", "fetch" for "go get and bring back", "bide" for "stay." Find others, and with your teacher's help try to explain where the word came from, and whether it was local slang, or a word from some far away place or time.

2. The qualities mentioned in the introduction are good qualities to be found in people. Do you think they are sufficient for a full life in today's world? What other qualities, if any, would you add to the list?

3. Why did Tom Topsail feel like a murderer as he chopped up the boat for wood for the fire? Did a boat mean more then, than it does now?

Things To Do

1. Draw a sketch of the ice field that the men became trapped in.

2. Do you suppose this was a rare event in the life of the Newfoundland sealer? Tell about similar dangerous incidents which you know of.

* * *

Getting Ready To Read

There are so many activities and interests which attract young people and adults outside the home that the family as a social unit hardly gets a chance to operate any more. At least, that seems to be the opinion of Louise in this selection. She sets out to make sure that her family has at least one evening when they can talk to each other and enjoy each other's company. See if you can identify the various factors which work against her intention.

This is part of a longer play written for radio by Helen Porter. Because it is not intended that the characters and action be seen, the play contains a greater emphasis on sound, using it to carry the action, to suggest atmosphere, and to bridge time from one scene to the next.

Notice the distinctions among the characters, and the simple conflicts which are part of most families.

A Quiet Evening At Home

Condensed Version

Characters:

Louise	Jack's Wife
Jack	Louise's Husband
Bob, Beth, Tony, Jan	Their Children

Setting:

The Squires' home near St. John's. Louise is alone, trying to catch up on some housework.

SOUND: TELEPHONE RINGS

LOUISE: Hallo. Oh, yes, Isabel. Yes, I did get a notice about it. No, I don't intend to go. I'm just too busy, girl. I was out every night for two weeks. What was I doing? Well, let's see. First it was the concert for the trawlermen, and then it was the protest down to City Hall. Yeah, about the high rise. No, I know we didn't get anywhere, but....Then, after that the Driver Safety Committee had meetings with the Minister, only he was too sick to attend....Well, they said he was *sick*, that's all I know. Oh yes, we were out picketing with the telephone operators, that's right. What a dirty deal. And mostly because they're women, you know. And then, after that, there was the education conference, and I ate potato salad at the banquet and was in bed for three days with food poisoning. (PAUSE) No, girl, the rest didn't really do me any good. You can imagine what the house was like when I got up. Oh, yes, the youngsters kept asking me if there was anything they could *do* for me. They asked me that several times, usually while they were tripping over the garbage or wondering where they could find some clean cups. So I've absolutely *promised* myself that I'm not going to get involved in anything else for a while. (PAUSE) No, girl, I can't go tonight, and that's that. We've decided to stay in tonight, all of us. It's ages since we've done that. Sorry about the meeting, but I'll try to make the next one. Okay then. 'Bye.

SOUND: RECEIVER BEING REPLACED

LOUISE: Oh Gosh, look at the time! They'll soon be home for supper and I haven't even got the place vacuumed.

SOUND: VACUUM, LOUD. TELEPHONE RINGS

LOUISE: Hallo. Sorry, I can't hear you. Oh, it's you, Jan. What are you whispering for? That's a bit better. No, I forgot all about making your appointment. Why don't you make it yourself? Well, if you've got time to 'phone me you've got time to 'phone Dr. Andrews. Don't know what to say? Listen, are you a university student or a kindergarten drop-out? Well, okay then, I'll do it tomorrow. What's for supper — oh, fish, I guess, fried fillet. No, I'm not going to get time to make a white sauce. Now, listen, you're not going out tonight, are you? It's ages since we've all been in together. Okay, see you then.

SOUND: RECEIVER BEING REPLACED
SOUND: TELEPHONE RINGS

LOUISE: Oh, no, not again. (VACUUM SOUND STOPS) Hallo. No, this is *not* the furniture department. I don't care what number you dialed, this is *not* K-Mart. Good*bye.*

SOUND: RECEIVER BEING REPLACED, HARD.

SOUND: VACUUM. FADE OUT

FADE IN TO CONVERSATION AND SUPPER NOISES

BOB: Got any dessert, Mom?

LOUISE: I made a couple of lemon pies but I don't know what they're like. Some of the yolk got into the white when I was making the meringue.

BOB: You know I don't like lemon. It's the only kind I don't like and you're always havin' it.

LOUISE: Bob, the last time I had it was three months ago.

BETH: This is the first time you've been in long enough to make one since then.

LOUISE: I thought you were supposed to be for women's liberation, Beth, with your Why Not button and your Ms magazines. It's all right as long as it doesn't apply to your own mother, is it?

BETH: Oh, Mom, stop tryin' to start something. I was only kidding.

JACK: Where's Tony? I haven't seen him for about two days.

LOUISE: Now, Jack, that's not true. You drove him up to school this morning. But does anyone know where he is now? I put his dinner in the oven.

BOB: He's up the road playin' street hockey. Mrs. Winterwate was in her door bawlin' them all out when I was comin' home.

LOUISE: Oh, my, not again. She 'phoned me the other day and I couldn't shut her up. Said she was going to 'phone the police if the boys didn't quit playing round her property.

BOB: Crabby old crow! Now, Dad, don't do that to your eyebrows. You know she is.

JACK: I don't know any such thing. She's had her basement window broken twice, you know. And if I find out Tony is saucing her back I'll....

LOUISE: Now, Jack, don't you go meeting trouble halfway again. He's not saucing her back. Have a piece of pie, now, and I'll put the kettle on for your coffee.

JACK: Did you put all the hot water in the teapot *again*?

LOUISE: Yes, but don't worry, it won't take a minute. You shouldn't be drinking so much coffee, anyhow. Bad for the heart.

SOUND: CLUMPING FOOTSTEPS. THEN DOOR OPENS AND CLOSES NOISILY

LOUISE: (CALLING) Is that you, Tony? Don't forget to take off your boots.

JACK: And get the hockey sticks out of the hall. Place looks like the Caps' dressing-room.

BOB: Smells like it, too.

TONY: You shut up, Bob. (PAUSE) Whaddaya got for supper, Mom?

LOUISE: Fish.

TONY: Yuck, not again. Can I have potted meat sandwiches?

LOUISE: Your supper is in the oven, Tony. And you're eating it, too. I'm too soft, that's what's wrong with you all.

TONY: Is there any gravy?

LOUISE: You don't have gravy with fish, Tony.

TONY: Up to Jim's they do.

LOUISE: Well, this is not Jim's Snacks, though sometimes it feels like it.

BETH: What's all this about staying in tonight, Mom? I promised Karen I might go up.

JAN: And I was going to the library to study.

LOUISE: Can't you stay in one night, just one? Is that too much to ask?

BOB: Gee, Mom, you're the one who's always out.

JACK: Bob, watch your tongue now.

BOB: Gee, I only said gee, Dad. If Mom can say heavens, why can't I say gee?

JACK: See? I told you what'd happen, didn't I?

LOUISE: I'm beginning to remember *why* I go out every night.

BETH: Oh, Mom, don't tell me you're going to give up on it before you even start. I was looking forward to staying home tonight, really. I only said that about going up to Karen's for badness. I was reading this book by O. Douglas, *Eliza for Common*, it's called. O. Douglas was really John Buchan's sister, did you know that?

JACK: *I* did.

LOUISE: Of course you did. *You* know everything.

BOB: But what's that got to do with staying in?

BETH: Well, that family, the Laidlaws, they all have such lovely times together. They sit home in the evenings, and the father reads to them all while the mother darns and....

BOB: I can just see Mom darning. Last time she tried it she sewed the sock on to her hand.

LOUISE: Shut up. And is there any reason on earth why a woman should automatically know how to darn any more than a man should? Talk about lip service to the women's movement....

BOB: Don't you mean lib service, Mom?

BETH: I wasn't finished talking about *Eliza for Common*. They all sit around, and Mary from Skye makes toast, and....

LOUISE: If I had a Mary from Skye I'd sit around too.

JACK: No, you wouldn't. You'd be afraid you were exploiting the lower classes.

LOUISE: Could anyone be lower class than us?

BETH: You can't get a chance to talk around here.

LOUISE: Go on, Beth. Don't mind them.

BOB: Them? You're worse than any of *us*.

LOUISE: What a way to talk to your mother. I wouldn't think of doing such a thing when I was a girl.

BOB: Oh, no. Don't try to fool *us*. Nanny Parsons told us all about you.

LOUISE: (TRAGICALLY) Got my own mother turned against me now, have you?

TONY: What happens after Mary-from-Space or whatever her name is makes toast?

BETH: Well, Tony, sometimes they sing an old Scottish ballad, and Mr. Laidlaw plays the penny whistle, and....

JACK: I had a nice little whistle once but someone got ahold of it and I never saw it again.

LOUISE: Will you ever forget that? I'll buy you ten whisles if you'll shut up about that one.

JACK: You can't hold on to anything in this house.

JAN: All that about the Laidlaws sounds great to me, Beth. Especially if we can have the television off.

BOB: Dad is the one always turns it on, anyhow.

TONY: But hockey is on tonight.

JACK: It's not going to hurt you to miss hockey for once. You're not supposed to see it on school nights, anyhow. You're hockey mad. It's about time for you to get your mind on something else.

BETH: Anyhow, what about it, Mom?

LOUISE: What about what?

BETH: Having the TV off and everything. We can play a game of Rook and....

BOB: I forget how.

BETH: And Dad can make popcorn, and Tony can go down the store to get some Pepsi.

JACK: I thought spending money would have to come into it somewhere.

LOUISE: Honestly, Jack. It's a good thing you're not as mean as you make out. But the whole idea sounds great to me, Beth, especially if I don't have to darn. It's time we spent a quiet evening at home.

JACK: Whose turn is it to do the dishes?

BETH & JAN: Bob and Tony's.

BOB: I got a lot of homework.

TONY: I got to go up to Jeff's to get my shoulder pads.

LOUISE: Beth, you and Jan do them tonight, will you?

BETH: It's a funny thing how often the girls in this house end up doing the dishes. Mom can talk all night at a meeting about sexism in schoolbooks but when it comes to her own family....

LOUISE: I notice neither one of you got dishpan hands yet. If you knew what it was to do as many dishes as I've done....

BOB: (SINGING) Ivory *Liquid*.

LOUISE: If you've got homework to do, do it, or I'll stick you at the sink after all.

JAN: The only time Bob ever thinks about homework is when someone asks him to do something.

TONY: Can I watch Police Story before we start being a cosy family?

JACK: Get at that homework before I cosy family you.

JAN: Beth and I have assignments to do too, you know.

LOUISE: (WITH GREAT RESIGNATION) Okay, I'll do the dishes myself. I'd rather get it over with than argue all night.

JACK: No, you won't, Louise. That's what's got these children like they are.

BETH: Why don't you do them, Dad?

JACK: I did them last night.

LOUISE: Well, will someone do them (PHONE RINGS) before I go stark, raving mad?

SOUND: PHONE RINGS, SEVERAL TIMES

JACK: Will someone please answer that phone?

BOB: Hallo. Pardon? No, it's not. At least I don't think so. Wait a minute, I'll check. Hey, Mom, someone wants to know if this is the Mental Hospital.

LOUISE: Bob, you stop that foolishness or I'll come out there and give you a shock treatment.

BOB: No, I'm sorry, you've got the wrong number. This is the Squires' Nuthouse.

FADE OUT
FADE IN
DISH NOISES/CONVERSATION

LOUISE: Well, here we all are. Isn't this nice? The television off, the corn all ready to pop, and everyone sitting around together. If we had a fireplace we could even have a fire in.

JACK: Want me to bring up the Coleman stove?

LOUISE: Jack, I'm just going to ignore you.

BETH: The corn will soon be popping. Is Tony going down the store?

TONY: Why am I always the one to go down the store? I'd drop dead if Jan ever went down. Were you ever down the store in your life, Jan?

JAN:	I was down the store before you were born, you little brat.
TONY:	Well, I'm sure you weren't down since.
JAN:	Now, Tony, you just shut up, or I'll....
LOUISE:	Is that the way Eliza for Common talks to her brothers?
BETH:	*Her* brothers are not like him.
JACK:	Will you stop picking at each other? I'm trying to read the paper and I can't concentrate.
BETH:	Do you want anything down the store, Dad?
JACK:	Hmm, let me see. Well, I suppose I could eat a plain milk bar.
BOB:	Bad for your teeth, Dad.
JACK:	Well, Bob, *you* don't have to pay the bill.
JAN:	Where's Tony *now?*
TONY:	(CALLING FROM HALL) I'm out here 'phonin' Jeff. Hallo, is that you, Jeff? Are you watchin' hockey tonight? Well, listen, I'll be 'phonin' you once in a while to get the score, okay? Not allowed to watch hockey here. 'Bye.
LOUISE:	Oh, Tony, what will Jeff's mother think we are?
BETH:	Relax, Mom and forget about that. Who cares, anyhow?
SOUND:	CORN POPPING LOUDLY
BETH:	Oh, heavens, I forgot about the popcorn.
JAN:	Tony, will you *please* go down the store?
TONY:	Okay, Brian.
JACK:	Brian? Who in heaven's name is *Brian?*

FADE OUT ON CORN POPPING.

Helen Porter

Recognition as a writer occurred for Helen Porter when she entered a play in the Newfoundland Arts and Letters competition and won first prize. Since then she has built a provincial and national reputation. Her many stories and essays have been published in Canadian and overseas magazines. She has selections in **Baffles of Wind and Tide, Doryloads,** *and* **From This Place.** *Her latest publication is* **Below the Bridge**, *a book describing life on the Southside of St. John's during the thirties and forties. She is presently living in Mount Pearl near St. John's.*

Persons wishing to perform the play publicly are asked to contact the author.

Understanding What You Have Read

1. What is the reaction of each character to Louise's suggestion that they stay at home?

2. Would there have been a better way to plan for an evening together?

3. What social concerns and issues are referred to in this excerpt? Choose one and list arguments related to it.

Things To Do

1. Discuss the best way to have this play come to life in the classroom. Select a cast and perform it. Don't forget the sound effects.

2. Write a stage version of this radio script.

3. Obtain a copy of the full play from your library, or from Helen Porter at 10 Penmore Drive in Mount Pearl, and enjoy the whole play.

4. Read "Confessions of a Hockey Mother" also by Helen Porter in *Doryloads* edited by Kevin Major. Compare the subject of that story to Tony in this play.

* * *

Jim Winter

FOREBEARS

II

The Darker Side

Newfoundland's history is punctuated with tragedies of epidemics, starvation, and death from drowning, freezing, fire and war. Although in the histories of all nations there are tragedies, it seems that Newfoundland's story has more dark passages than the stories of most other nations.

To truly understand your past — the times and lives of your ancestors — you have to read and hear the hard, sad times endured and overcome. Only then can you fully understand and appreciate why Ray Guy would say with truth, "Your average Newfoundlander is waterproof, dustproof, shock-resistant and anti-magnetic....He has been bred, over three or four hundred years, for durability. Endurance is his secret."

Getting Ready To Read

As a preparation for the following selection it might be a good idea to read three short selections from *Doryloads* which provide a background to the seal hunt as it used to be: "Seal Hunting Song"; "From The Log of Bob Bartlett"; and "Elegy for Lost Sealers".

In "The *Greenland* Disaster", Gerald Jones gives the factual details of the great tragedy. This piece of writing could be almost a newspaper report except for the subjective (author point of view) touches such as the quotes of the dying men and Mr. Jones' personal feelings.

The *Greenland* Disaster

It was a sad spring day in 1908 when the sealing vessel *Greenland* sailed into St. John's Harbor with her cargo of twenty five frozen bodies and news of twenty three others lost on the ice fields. That day many a strong man shed tears as thousands stood around the waterfront to witness this chamber of horrors as the lifeless cargo was unloaded and tales of misery told. Their story was rated as one of the most remembered of all Newfoundland marine tragedies.

The *Greenland* sailed with the rest of the fleet out of St. John's Harbor on March 10, 1908, heading north to where the seals were thought to be. She passed inside the Funks on March 13 and encountered the heavy Arctic floe, seventy miles beyond the islands, and was joined by other members of the fleet, *Neptune, Walrus, Leopard, Diana, Aurora, Iceland* and *Mastiff.* The weather was cold and unsettled, an indication of the storms that were to come.

On the thirteenth, the *Greenland* struck the first patch of young harps and for a week cruised about, killing and panning seals and hauling them on board.

On the fifteenth a gale raged while the men were on the ice and they were unable to reach the safety of the ship until midnight.

The ice was in long, heavy unbroken sheets and the ship ran along its outer edges. Jason Gaulton's watch of fifty men was put over the side and two miles further on, the watches of Jesse

Knee, Nat House and Jason Morris were sent off, one hundred and fifty four men in all, just at dawn. Shortly after dropping the last two watches, the ship headed back to the first watch for the barometer was dropping and there was little doubt that a storm was brewing.

With Jason Gaulton's watch safely on board, the *Greenland* headed back for the main company of men. She couldn't make it for the wind had changed and rafted the ice before the ship into an impenetrable* barrier a mile across and several feet thick. Beyond was a channel of water two or three miles across, on the farther side of which were gathered the sealers, as powerless to reach the steamer as she was to reach them.

The wind came up fast in hurricane force. The small boats could not be hauled across the ice barrier and launched into the water on the other side for it would mean death to their crews. The only hope was that the men on the ice might get picked up by one of the other steamers in the vicinity.

That Monday night, according to the captain and crew aboard the *Greenland*, a gale blew like none ever before experienced. Though well freighted with seals and coal, the ship was blown over until her leeward yards were level with the floe and her deck load of coal and provisions shot into the ice scuppers* and threatened to turn her bottom up. All night the wind raged and all night the crew struggled to keep the ship in trim.

On Monday when the gale sprang up the men stranded on the ice gathered in a body to discuss how to make the best of their desperate situation. Seven or eight parties were formed, and were started off to different points of the compass in the hope that one would soon strike a ship. But the storm became their barrier.

The parties led by Jesse Knee and navigator William Davis built shelters of snow and ice and huddled together in them to pass the night.

About 10 p.m. the first man died, Alfred Newtry, a stowaway, a young lad of eighteen from Carbonear.

Through the night the storm raged and the hungry men wandered about in every direction. Many fell through fissures* and seal blowholes in the ice.

Henry Lush from Greenspond, a seasoned sealer, was with a body of about fifty sealers. He saw many men drop down and die.

George Tuff, seventeen, from Newton, was in Jesse Knee's watch. "When the storm came up we divided into two squads," he said, "it was snowing and blowing like I had never seen before. The two squads of men were about two gunshots apart. Some of the men grew weak. The first to die was George Pynn, twenty seven, from Harbor Grace who was followed soon by Richard Pynn, nineteen, from St. John's. When daylight broke five dead men lay with us.

"Tuesday all kinds of queer fancies ran through my mind and I saw houses, trees, gardens and other beautiful sights. On attempting to raise a limb I would fall to the ice. Some died raving that the steamer was close by; others in their efforts to save brothers and relatives gave up their own lives."

Few others would have died had not Samuel Burry become insane and rushed among the men shouting that the ship was cominng toward them. Men ran searching for the ship and were soon lost sight of while others, on finding the ship wasn't coming, deliberately walked into the water and others lay on the ice to die.

On Tuesday morning G. Ryan of Harbor Grace fell into the water but was pulled out by several men nearby. He ran and jumped for a couple of hours until, exhausted, he dropped to the ice and died almost immediately.

Henry Stagg of Cape Freels remembered seeing two men fall to the ice and perish.

About 4 p.m. Tuesday afternoon the gale abated and a small group of half-dead men gathered along the ice front as the *Greenland* bore down on them.

Men from the *Greenland* quickly swarmed onto the flow and made their way among the stricken sealers. The joy of rescue was too much for many and they dropped dead just as the rescuers reached them.

The *Greenland* was joined by the *Iceland* and *Diana*, which abandoned seal-killing to assist the stricken ship. They searched until darkness rendered further searching impossible but early Wednesday the search resumed for the fifty four men still missing.

After two nights of agony on the treacherous floe even the boldest spirits succumbed and on Wednesday only six of the fifty four were found alive.

One of the six picked up on Wednesday was Alfred Gaulton, a lad of eighteen. He had spent forty eight hours on the ice. Twice on Monday night he lay down to die, but death refused to come. He was picked up, mentally deranged, by some relatives on Wednesday afternoon.

Phineas Stokes of Cape Freels was taken aboard the *Greenland* Tuesday and only then in the warmth of the ship did he realize how badly frozen he was.

On Friday the *Greenland* was thirty miles off Cape Bonavista and as another severe gale was raging she put into Bay de Verde and wired to St. John's. That evening, the storm, which seemed to follow the ship, again burst in all its fury. As the night wore on the storm increased in fury and although riding at anchor with sixty fathoms of chain out, the ship could not stand the strain and the anchor snapped at midnight. A full head of steam was kept up but soon she began to drift and suddenly she struck bottom. All hands thought that at any moment she would go under and take both living and dead with her. Coal shifting was at once resorted to with the result that after five hours in a dangerous predicament she was floated and left for St. John's with the loss of part of her keel.

But the trouble was not yet over. In the dense fog off Cape St. Francis she narrowly escaped running on the Biscay rocks.

At 7:30 p.m. Saturday, March 26, the first news of the sealing tragedy reached St. John's. At 3 p.m. Sunday the *Greenland* arrived in St. John's and the restless thousands of people from the city gathered at Baine Johnston's wharf.

Charles Weeks, a shopkeeper, jumped on the *Greenland* as she touched the wharf, looking for his brother Jack of Wesleyville. He was told by Jason Gaulton, the master watch, that Jack was missing.

The government had provided everything possible for the emergency and Governor Murray, Premier Winter, Colonial Secretary Robinson and nearly every member of the

Legislature were present to give whatever assistance was possible.

Newfoundlanders were men of the sea, from families who lived from the sea, and the pain and agony of tragedies at sea was nothing new to them. The *Greenland* disaster, as other sealing disasters before it, burned scars on people's memories but still, next spring, men will come into St. John's to fight for a berth* on a sealing ship.

Gerald Jones

Understanding What You Have Read

1. List some things which indicate that the sealers were poorly equipped for storm conditions.

2. List some events or conditions which contributed to the tragedy.

3. Reread the last paragraph of the selection. What does it tell you about the kind of person the Newfoundland sealer was? Describe him fully.

Things To Do

1. Read *Death on the Ice* by Cassie Brown.

2. Try to get some information on today's seal hunt. Write to the Provincial Department of Fisheries for details of conditions aboard sealing ships today.

3. Compare your findings with the descriptions in "The *Greenland* Disaster" and *Death on the Ice.*

* * *

A Sealer ("Greenland" Class)

Getting Ready To Read

E.J. Pratt was a Newfoundland poet who became one of Canada's best known writers. Although he spent most of his adult life in Ontario, he often wrote about the sea and about the effect of the forces of nature on people.

The poem "Erosion" contains two sentences, each forming a stanza identical in poetic structure to the other. That is, the lines have the same rhythm, and the stanzas have the same rhyme scheme.

The literal meaning of erosion is the process by which nature moves and shapes the materials of the earth. You will find this literal meaning of erosion in stanza one. The figurative meaning of erosion is any process which acts to change or shape a person, a feeling or a relationship. You will find this figurative meaning of erosion in stanza two. Notice how Pratt suggests the personality of the sea by reference to its "tracing" or "placing" things, as if it had hands.

Erosion

It took the sea a thousand years,
A thousand years to trace
The granite feature of this cliff,
In crag* and scarp* and base.

It took the sea an hour one night,
An hour of storm to place
The sculpture of these granite seams
Upon a woman's face.

E.J. Pratt

Edwin John Pratt was born in Western Bay, Newfoundland, in 1883, and in 1907 he moved to Toronto where he attended

Victoria College. His talents as a writer were recognized and developed so that eventually he became the unofficial poet laureate of Canada. Much of his great narrative poetry was written on such topics as the national railway, the early missionaries in Canada, immense struggles between creatures of the deep, and the great tragedy of the loss of the **Titanic**. *His early poetry, however, is set in Newfoundland and contains Newfoundland images and experiences. Many of these are found in* **Newfoundland Verse** *(1923),* **The Witches Brew** *(1925) and* **Collected Poems** *(1944). The poems "Erosion," "Sea Gulls" and "The Lee Shore" are regarded as masterpieces of lyric expression. Dr. Pratt died in 1964, assured of his place in world literature.*

Understanding What You Have Read

1. What is the stanza containing the main poetic idea? What is the purpose of the other stanza?

2. How is the word "granite" used in stanza two as compared with its use in stanza one?

Things To Do

1. Get a copy of *Openings*; read "The Lee-Shore" also by E.J. Pratt. How are the poems similar in content? How are they different in structure?

2. Write a paragraph about what you think was happening in stanza two. What human emotions are suggested but not stated?

* * *

Getting Ready To Read

"Newfoundland may well feel proud of its sons. The heroism and devotion to duty they displayed on 1st July has never been surpassed." So wrote Field- Marshall Sir Douglas Haig in tribute to the seven hundred and ten Newfoundlanders who died in the Battle of Beaumont Hamel on July 1, 1916. On that day ninety per cent of the Newfoundland Regiment was wiped out in an attempt to break through the enemy lines. They failed, but their heroism earned for the Newfoundland Regiment the title "The Fighting Newfoundlanders."

The story, "The Caribou", is set at Beaumont Hamel. A father and his son, John and Richard, have driven from France to Beaumont Hamel and when their car breaks down with a flat tire,Richard takes the opportunity to view the battlegrounds of World War I around Beaumont Hamel. A stranger mysteriously appears in their midst. He accurately describes for Richard the Battle of Beaumont Hamel — or the July Drive, as the Newfoundlanders call it. Then mysteriously, he is gone. Who was he? If you read "The Caribou" slowly and carefully, you will be aware of the curiosity and suspense the writer builds within you. This, you will notice, is accomplished by the description of the landscape, the stranger, Richard's unusual behavior, and by the surprise ending. What really did happen to John's car?

The Caribou

"What's that?" asked Richard. At the summit of the mount, about thirty feet above their heads, stood a massive statue of an animal like a reindeer.

"I haven't a clue," replied his father irritably. He was tired. It had not been a good idea to take the night-ferry over the Channel. It had been still less of a good idea to allow the boy to do the navigating on the road. He had been persuaded out of taking the motor-way route: for no good reason Richard had suggested in Arras that they should take the country roads and he had agreed. Now here they were stranded a few miles short of Albert at half past seven in the morning and not a soul in sight.

It was perhaps lucky that the near-side front tyre had chosen to blow out outside this part of whatever it was. The car had ground to a halt just by the inset semi-circular bay that enclosed the gravelled opening. French country roads are narrow and it could have been awkward if one of those big tractors had come trundling* along whilst they were changing the wheel.

He had climbed out of the car wearily and, glancing across the road to a gentle valley which lay drowsing in the early morning sunshine, had noticed a tall white cross on the downward slope. It was surrounded by uniform rows of grey head-stones. He had meant to point out this First World War cemetary to Richard, but Richard had wandered off inside the gateway and was staring up at a green bank. In this, just above eye-level, was a crimson triangle set in a bronze oblong. Below it was a plaque stating that it was in memory of the men of the Twenty-ninth Division. Beyond the low mound was a belt of trees. They had walked through these and had come out on to an open green space which was dominated by the tall mound, on top of which stood the huge animal statue. It was facing the rising sun in an attitude, not exactly defiant*, but somehow challenging.

John blinked in the early morning sunlight. There was a slight mist, but the cloudless sky promised a day of scorching heat. Ahead of them was a trench: it was covered with grass, very neatly clipped, but it was undoubtedly a trench. John focussed his eyes on the slope beyond. It was pitted with small depressions, grass-grown like the trench.

"Shell-holes," he said to Richard. "This must be one of those parts of the Western Front they preserved as a memorial. They did that up on Vimy Ridge I believe."

But Richard was not listening. He was walking slowly along the top of the grass-grown trench. He crossed the top of it by a plank-bridge and, carefully skirting the shell-holes, made his way down the slope. John had a sudden strange feeling that there was an incredible distance between them, as though time had slipped, and he and Richard were in two different dimensions. He plodded off down the slope to catch him up.

They had gone about six hundred yards when they came to another grassy ditch with a black and white sign that said "German Front Line." To their right was a beautiful small cemetery marked Y Ravine. There was the stone Cross of Sacrifice with its reversed bronze sword, and around it the neat rows of white head-stones with pink wild roses fluttering against them.

A short distance behind the trench was Y Ravine itself. It was a deep sudden cleft in the earth, as though Nature herself had taken to digging trenches. But this natural feature was a good thirty feet deeper than the man-made ditches on the slope. They gazed silently down into its shadowed depths, and then turned to go up to the slope again.

Past a little belt of trees there was yet another cemetary. It was called Hawthorn Ridge N.1 and it was much bigger than Y Ravine cemetery on the other side of the park.

They went back to the memorial and climbed up the narrow path that wound its way round the shrub-covered eminence.*

"I wonder what happened here?" said Richard as they reached the top.

"A whole battalion set out to march down that slope and were shot to pieces before they had covered a hundred yards of it," said another voice. John felt neither startled nor surprised — it was as though he had been expecting someone to provide an answer. He turned to look at the newcomer.

Standing about a couple of yards away on the path behind was a tall young man with very bright brown eyes. He was about six feet two, John estimated, and not all that young — late twenties perhaps.

"They were the First Battalion, the Newfoundland Regiment," he continued. "On this very day, first of July, in 1916 they went over the top. That's their memorial up there — the regimental symbol, a caribou."

"Where's his accent?" John wondered to himself. "It's not American. It's not Canadian either. There was a Canadian battery training near us in 1942 and they didn't sound quite like that. I'll ask him where he's from."

But before he could formulate the question, the stranger

was speaking again. "See down there where it says British Front Line? Well, there were rows of barbed wire in front of that, and in the nights before the Big Drive they cut gaps in it so the attacking troops could go through. There were three brigades in the 29th Division — 86th on the left there, 87th on the right beyond those trees and the 88th in support. The Newfoundlanders were in the support brigade, the 88th. That's their trench — where it says St. John's Road. It's a communication trench, runs back to Auchonvillers. They formed up in that on 30th June and waited their turn to move. They were the third wave; their job was to pass through the first and second waves when these had taken their objectives and go on to take the last line of German defences. Then the cavalry would ride through to Bapaume, the German line would be rolled up and that was to be the end of the whole messy business. Victory — peace — everyone could go back home again." He surveyed the sunlit slope below.

"I wonder why he calls the battle the Big Drive?" thought John. "The British called it the Big Push or the Great Attack."

Richard broke the short silence. "What did happen?" he asked.

The bright eyes remained fixed on the slope. "At twenty-five past seven the first four battalions climbed out of their trenches. They didn't get far. Remember those gaps I told you about in the defensive wire? The men had to bunch together to pass through those and the Germans had machine-guns trained on the gaps. There was some shelling, of course, but there were an awful lot of machine-guns: it was the machine-guns did most of the damage. Some of the men got through on to the slope but shrapnel* bursts and rifle fire did for them. Then the second wave were on the move, but they were hampered by the dead and wounded from the first wave and they only added to the khaki heaps on the ground.

"At nine-fifteen the Colonel got the order that the Newfoundlanders were to advance. And so they did. They couldn't move through the communication trenches to the front line — these were all jammed with wounded. So they went out of St. John's Road above ground to the front line, and through the gaps as best they could and out into No Man's

Land. They went as steadily as though they were on parade. The only sign that they were aware of the hail of bullets flying at them was that they put their heads down and tucked their chins into their shoulders, as they used to do when fighting their way through a blizzard in the outports back home. Half an hour later there wasn't one of them standing. About seven hundred and eighty men went down that slope: seven hundred and ten of them became casualties."

He pointed to some small bronze arrows set in the low wall that guarded the path. "See those? They point to places especially important to the Newfoundlanders. This one says Danger Tree. That's the Danger Tree halfway down the hill. That's about as far as any of them got."

His voice died away as he and Richard moved down the circular path to the bottom of the mound. John followed slowly. "That man is like the Ancient Mariner," he thought to himself. "It's as though he's forced to tell this dreadful tale."

His hand, resting on the low stone wall, encountered something suddenly cold. It was one of the bronze arrows, rather larger than the others and pointing north-westward. The lettering on it read: "Newfoundland 2500 miles." John walked thoughtfully on down to the bottom of the mound.

In the sunshine, beside an old white, dead stump of a tree beyond the lines of grassy trenches, Richard and the stranger were talking earnestly together. John turned to look at the bronze caribou high above his head, silhouetted* against the blue sky. He glanced down at his watch. It was quarter past nine.

Then suddenly Richard was on the path beside him again.

"He seemed a nice chap," said John as they walked back to the entrance. "Where did he come from?"

He looked round the sunlit park; it seemed quite empty. "And where did he go?" he added.

"Said his name was Richard — like me," replied the boy. "He went in there." Richard pointed towards the small iron gate that led into Y Ravine cemetery. John could see the tall cross, but the small plot was a fair distance away and it was shaded by trees: certainly he could not see anyone.

"Hadn't we better change that tyre?" Richard asked

abruptly and moved away to the back of the car and got out the tool-kit.

John stooped down to examine the offending wheel. "Those tyres were almost new when we started," he grumbled. "Must have picked up a nail or a sliver of glass or something."

Then he stared unbelievingly. In the wall of the tyre were three neatly-spaced round holes — like the holes machine-gun bullets make.

Joy B. Cave

Joy Cave is an English teacher at the Priory Grammar School for Girls in Shrewsbury, England, where she was born. While serving in the Women's Auxiliary Air Force during World War II she met many Newfoundlanders, and from these associations grew a love for Newfoundland, which she has visited time and again. Her abiding affection for Newfoundland is revealed in her story of the Royal Newfoundland Regiment in World War I: **What Became of Corporal Pittman?**

Understanding What You Have Read

1. Where are Richard and John stranded and at what hour in the morning? Why are they stranded? Where did the stranger come from?

2. a) What question does the stranger answer for Richard? Describe the stranger.
   b) What does John notice about the accent of the stranger? With what accent, do you think, the stranger spoke?

3. How does the stranger know so much about what happened on July 1, 1916? (The answer to this question is not stated. You have to guess it from what happens in the story.)

4. What surprises Richard and John about the flat tire?

Things To Do

1. Joy Cave uses a very extensive vocabulary in "The Caribou." Check the meanings of the following words in the glossary at the back or in a dictionary. Now write sentences in which you correctly use any five words from the following list.

   summit
   irritably
   trundling
   oblong
   eminence
   shrapnel
   silhouetted

2. John described the stranger as being "like the Ancient Mariner". Who was the Ancient Mariner? How was the stranger like him?

3. Write a story dealing with the supernatural.

4. Find out from your parents, relatives, or from members of the Canadian Legion, or from a war veteran, what part individuals from your area played in the Great Wars.

5. With the help of your librarian or your teacher find a copy of Joy Cave's book *What Became of Corporal Pittman?* You may also be interested in other accounts of the Royal Newfoundland Regiment in action. Your librarian can help you.

* * *

The Caribou — Beaumont Hamel Park

Picnic at Pearce's Field, Forest Pond, c. 1898

FOREBEARS

Part III

The Lighter Side

Just as the moon has a dark side and a light side, so do our lives. But in having the sad or dark times we appreciate and enjoy more fully the happy times.

Our forebears reacted to the darker side and the lighter side equally well. They mourned at funerals but they celebrated at weddings. They sang and joked at Christmas time and at dances and times, concerts and parties of all descriptions. There really were times to laugh, and our ancestors knew how to take full advantage of them, as you will see in the essays and the folksong which are found in this unit.

Getting Ready To Read

This is an essay, a personal remembering, of what Christmas was like in a Newfoundland outport during the nineteen forties. It is particularly effective because the author, Ray Guy, gives so many details, and because he uses appeals to all five senses. He particularly appeals to the senses of sight, taste and smell.

Although the essay is about Christmas, you should notice that Mr. Guy gives a lot of details of everyday living as well. He is most concerned with the people. Be aware of his attention to so many different types of people, some directly, some indirectly. Notice that he handles them, and what they do, very gently.

Christmas

In the last week of Advent* the house smelled like a forest.

Behind the kitchen stove, stacked as neatly as books on library shelves, was a wall of firewood. Some junks of dry and weathered rampikes* but most of sappy spruce and balsam fir with turpentine bladders and green twigs sticking off.

The heat from the stove brought out the smell. Out in the porch there were firewood reinforcements. The woodbox was full: it was piled high and at both ends.

In all, there was enough firewood in the house and ready to do, along with a few scuttles* of coal, for twelve nights.

Some say the artificial Christmas trees are disappointing because there's no smell on them. In the mid-nineteen-forties, Christmas trees were still uncommon out around the bay but you wouldn't have noticed the smell of one anyway for the aroma off the twelve-days' supply of firewood.

The kitchen stove was the only source of heat in the house. It was allowed to die out at night and was relit each morning with splits* and shavings.

Indeed, people passed every night of the winter in uninsulated houses with no fire, no storm windows. If it was ten degrees out of doors, by morning it could be ten degrees in the bedrooms.

They kept warm on mattresses stuffed with feathers and

down of chickens and wild birds, covered over with quilts and comforters stuffed with wool.

Now we have a fuel crisis and great countries are plunged into distress because thermostats have to be turned down to sixty-eight degrees.

Christmas lasted a whole twelve days then. It was the most remarkable celebration of the year. Even weddings did not come close to it.

Everything possible was done to see that work was cut to a bare minimum during these twelve days. Enough firewood was in and the water-barrels in the porch brimmed full of water from the well.

All the laundry, baking, scrubbing, butchering, brewing, polishing, mending, patching and cleaning had been done until seven days into the New Year.

The turkey wasn't invented yet but there were rabbits in the bakepot and turrs in the oven. There were fowls stewed tender with onions and stuffing and the carcass of a lamb or pig hanging down in the store over the water where it would keep.

There were ducks and geese and venison and salt water birds. There were herring and potatoes and bread. There was jam yesterday, today and tomorrow. There were candies and brew and brandy from St. Peter's.

And there was rum washed out of rum puncheons and wine in bottles from Madeira. There was lots of church, and the poles with the kerosene lamps on them on both sides of the aisle were wrapped in evergreen boughs and tissue-paper roses.

Christmas now is a glorified weekend. People then apparently determined to give themselves the whole twelve days because they knew they needed it. It was not coincidence that a hard-working people gave themselves the longest break of the year at such a time.

It is the darkest time of year; the long, hard winter stretches ahead. So why not shatter the darkness and gloom with a glorious bash that was the highlight of the year in those times and would be impossible to achieve in today's society.

Considering the circumstances, Christmas then was a heroically defiant thing, a blaze of light hurled by puny men against the longest night; a brazen riotous celebration to say that in the midst of darkness the Saviour was born and the people would live through the cold, both in body and soul.

It was a most positive and optimistic thing.

Ray Guy

Ray Guy is a widely-read Newfoundland journalist. Since the early 1960s, he has written for local newspapers and magazines, and more recently has appeared regularly in mainland publications. He has won two national awards for his writing, the most recent being the Stephen Leacock Award for Humour for **That Far Greater Bay** *published in 1976.*

Mr. Guy is a native of Arnold's Cove and is presently living in St. John's with his wife and children. Aside from his writing, Mr. Guy will be known to students as Jack, a character appearing in the CBC television series "Up At Ours."

Things To Do:

1. Read part or all of this essay to some older person in your family or community. Talk to them about some of their recollections.

2. We all know that Christmas is the time when the Church celebrates the birth of Jesus Christ. What is the significance of each of the following?

   a) Advent
   b) Twelve Days of Christmas
   c) St. Stephen's Day
   d) Old Christmas Day

3. Sketch one of the scenes so well described by Ray Guy.

4. Find at least one piece of description for each of the five senses.

* * *

Getting Ready To Read

Ray Guy recalls some of the enjoyable activities of his childhood in Arnolds Cove, and calls them "Outharbor Juvenile Delights." Sometimes the activities were not really enjoyable, but he still lists them as delights. You will find both kinds in this short essay. Remember that they are seen through the eyes of a child, and the curiosity of the child often overshadows the significance of the event.

Mr. Guy uses very interesting writing techniques in this essay. Notice his short descriptions of two enjoyable "delights" at the beginning, and then his use of the "ritual chants" as a bridge to take us into the more sombre ritual of funerals. His use of short and long sentence combinations helps to focus our attention on the point he wants us to consider. See how he gives the impression of many people saying the same thing one after the other in his description of the funeral. Note as well the emphasis given by use of short sentence fragments.

Finally, notice that he uses the ritual statements from both the funeral and the wedding to speak directly to us, wishing us, really, a Happy Spring!

The Rites of Spring

The springs were always ringing with ritual* chants*. Like in Playing Rings with a girl and a feller in the centre and the rest going around: "Now you're married I wish you much joy, every year a girl or a boy, if one don't do I wish you two, if two don't do I wish you three, if three don't do I wish you four, if four don't do I wish you no more, so take me outa me dory."

Funerals. There seemed always to be funerals in the spring. The ones who lost someone belonging to them would stand there and everyone would come in and go over and shake hands with them.

They didn't look at their faces. They would shake hands and murmur something to them and pass on, looking down or looking past them.

What did they say? They all said the same thing but it was hardly loud enough for anyone to hear. What did they say? I found out once when we lost someone belonging to us. I could hear it.

They all came in and shook hands and murmured and passed on without looking at our faces. And they all said: "Sorry for your trouble." "Sorry for your trouble." "...for your trouble." "Sorry...." That is what they said.

And the blinds down in the houses like white eyes, not looking. White not black. And the bell tolling slow. Slow. They had to go up to where the bell was in the belfry and tie a piece of cloth around the clapper and strike it against the bell with a line.

Even if the sun was shining the bell tolling put a white sheet over the whole day. Not black. White. White and sorry but immensely calm. Immensely.

Delight? Well, there are some things that always must be done. Do you know how it can be done better?

There seemed always to be weddings after Lent. George Albert blew a foot off the barrel of his father's britch loader at one wedding. Oh, yes. A wonder, you know, he wasn't killed or worse. But seeing it was a wedding his father let him off with it.

They used to be married in the church and hold the wedding in the schoolhouse which was done up for the same purpose.

I would say that three parts of the fellers getting married had a drop or two in. And there were some down in the back seats not too steady, either. I mean to say, not for a place of worship.

After the marriage all the people lined up and went past the bunch who were just married just like at the funerals. Well, not like at funerals, no.

They all muttered something to them as they went past, yes. And all the women giving the bride the big smackers and all the men shaking hands with the poor young feller in a robust fashion and shaking their heads at him.

And they all muttering something to them. All saying the same thing, pretty well. I was a hardy boy before I discovered what it was they all said.

Talk about brazen. Oh, yes, brazen as brass when there is something to be found out, although you'd never say it. I got behind the bunch who were just married once so I could hear what they were saying.

They all shook hands with them and said: "Wish you much joy." That is what they all were saying. "Wish you much joy."

A wonder it was that we didn't catch on to it before. But we thought we were only playing when we were Playing Rings. "Now you're married I wish you much joy...." And we only youngsters. You'd never think it, would you.

If it is coming on spring where you are, I must say to you since the time is in it, and while I remember. Sorry for your trouble. Wish you much joy.

Ray Guy

Understanding What You Have Read

1. A rite is a custom or activity which always accompanies a definite occasion or event. Why does Mr. Guy call the activities "Rites of Spring?" Does he use another word in the essay which suggests the same thing?

2. Can you find instances of alliteration in this essay? What effect does it have in each case?

3. Read aloud the paragraphs describing the sights and sounds accompanying the pulling down of the blinds in the houses and the tolling of the bell.

4. Notice the introductory sentences for the section describing funerals and the section concerned with weddings.

Things To Do

1. Think of some things which puzzled or confused you when you were a child and try to describe your impressions or observations at that time.

2. Read other "Outharbor Delights" in *You May Know Them As Sea Urchins Ma'am* and *That Far Greater Bay*, both by Ray Guy.

3. Ask older people about ritual chants from their childhood. Read pages 49 to 54 of *More Than 50%* by Hilda Chaulk Murray.

4. What is the movement referred to in the wedding reception as "shaking their heads at him." It is not an ordinary shake of the head, and has no negative meaning. This custom is still common in some parts of the British Isles and Newfoundland. What is the meaning?

5. Read the biographical note on Ray Guy found at the end of "Christmas" on page 58

* * *

Justin Hall

Getting Ready To Read

From reading "Babysittin' " you have learned that Ted Russell's narrative essays (essays that tell stories) are often very humorous. This humour is the result of exaggeration. Exaggeration is a favourite device for creating humour, and is popular not only among Newfoundland writers but among writers everywhere. Exaggeration occurs when the truth is stretched beyond belief. As you read "Football" observe how Russell exaggerates the actions and descriptions of his characters, especially the Noddy family, to create a humorous effect.

There's nothing like some new machine to create excitement amongst people. The first motor car or sea plane to come to a Newfoundland outport always created a bustle of excitement. In the bustle of excitement occurred many humorous actions and remarks. Well, according to Grampa Walcott, it was just "forty three years ago" that the first football (really a soccer ball) floated into Pigeon Inlet. The fuss caused by that bag of air was unbelievable and unforgettable. Football had come to Pigeon Inlet, and Pigeon Inlet, says Uncle Mose, was never the same again.

Football

Watchin' our Pigeon Inlet football team givin' the crowd from Hartley's Harbour such a lickin' every 24th of May, 'tis hard to believe that only fifty years ago, such a thing as football had never been seen or heard tell of in Pigeon Inlet. As a matter of fact, I wouldn't believe it myself only Grampa Walcott tells the story, and everyone knows he's a truthful man.

'Twas forty-three years ago last week, accordin' to Grampa, that Uncle Solomon Noddy was rowin' in from fishin' when he spotted this thing driftin' along just ahead of him. First he thought it was the head of a swile. But just then a flaw of wind lifted it right out of the water, so like he said after, he knowed it wasn't a swile's head 'cause there was nar a swile under it. Nor was it the head of a drowned man for the same reason. He rowed up closer and figgered that, unless it happened to be a

German bomb-shell, it'd come in handy for a trawl bobber. So he said a short prayer and picked it up. 'Twas laced up just like a boot, although he'd never seen anyone with a foot that shape. He shook it, but it seemed all hollow inside, so he figgered 'twas a trawl bobber sure enough, and he brought it in.

He carried it up to his house, showed it to Aunt Paish his missus and told her not to let young Jethro fool with it 'cause he wasn't sure yet but what it might be a bomb-shell after all. He laid it on a kitchen chair while he went back to put away his bit of fish. Young Jethro, says Grampa, was just a little nipper then about six or seven year old with a nasty temper and a dirty habit of kickin' at everything that didn't please him. Well, he come in from wherever he'd been out around the back yard — probably kickin' the cat — and spotted this thing on the kitchen chair. Aunt Paish was busy getting Uncle Sol's dinner ready and didn't notice anything until she heard him say, "Look, ma, it pops," and when she slewed* round from where she'd been bendin' over the stove, there was Jethro bouncin' this thing on the floor. Well it popped sure enough, right up agen young Jethro's nose, and before Aunt Paish could scravel over to stop him, he'd up foot and let this thing have it. Aunt Paish, says Grampa, never could describe exactly what happened for the next few minutes after that, but it could be pieced together by examinin' the wreckage later on.

It appears that this thing left young Jethro's boot and headed straight across the front of Aunt Paish's dresser where, like a tidy housekeeper, she had all her best jugs and cups hung on little hooks on the outside with the lower grade stuff in back on the shelves. Well, it swept the top row on the way over, bounced off the kitchen wall and took the other row on the way back. It smashed everything, includin' Uncle Sol's moustache cup with "Love the Giver" on it, that'd been in the Noddy family for three generations. The lifter was stickin' up out of the cover of the stove. It hit that, and sent it flyin' end on right through the half-gallon brown teapot that had just been set to brew on the back of the stove. So from then on the steam was so thick that Aunt Paish wasn't prepared to swear what it was that smashed the lamp and the motto with "God Bless our Happy Home" on it.

Anyway in the middle of it all, in come Uncle Sol lookin' for his dinner like a man would, and seen the mess. The fog was lightened just enough for him to see young Jethro and Aunt Paish pointin' to this thingamajig lyin' on the floor as harmless lookin' a thing as you'd care to see. 'Twas then Uncle Sol showed where it was young Jethro got his temper from. "Gimme the axe,"he bawled, "and I'll fix it."

So out he started into the back yard and come back with an axe, and a good job it was, said Grampa, that it wasn't a double bitter. 'Cause Uncle Sol bended over that thing where 'twas lyin' on the floor, swung the axe over his head, and brought it down as hard as he could. We'll never know, says Grampa, whether 'twas the axe or the other thing that bounced back and struck Uncle Sol right between the two eyes. Anyway, Aunt Paish dragged him outside into the fresh air where she thought he'd have a better chance of comin' to. Then she went back into the kitchen with her mind set on endin' this foolishness once and for all.

The thing was still lyin' there peaceful on the floor, so she grabbed it up, opened the end of the Waterloo stove, poked it in, and closed the door on it. Well, sir, says Grampa, the Hartley's Harbour people come hurryin' in off the fishin' grounds. They thought 'twas the smoke of the old Glencoe. And of course all the neighbours in Pigeon Inlet come runnin'.

That night after Uncle Sol had come to and the women had helped Aunt Paish clean up the mess, 'twas the general opinion it must have been a bomb-shell after all. And those of us, says Grampa, who liked to look at the brighter side of things couldn't help remarkin' how it had cured young Jethro of his habit of kickin' at things, besides givin' the Noddy chimney the first cleanin' out it had in years.

And it wasn't until two or three years afterwards that Aunt Paish was thumbin' through a catalogue up at Grandma Walcott's one night and what should she spy but a picture of the very thing that'd caused all the trouble. And now, says Grampa, not fifty years later, to think that our fellows trim the socks off the Hartley's Harbour crowd at football every 24th of May — reg'lar as clockwork.

Ted Russell

Understanding What You Have Read

1. Whom does Uncle Mose quote as the source for his story? Uncle Mose seems to have some doubts about the truth of the story, yet he believes what he heard. Why?

2. What did Uncle Solomon Noddy think the football was?

3. a) What did Jethro do with the football? With what results?
   b) What did Uncle Solomon try to do with the football? With what results?
   c) What did Aunt Paish do with the football? With what results?

4. In what ways could it be said that the football really was "a bombshell"?

Things To Do

1. Give several examples of exaggeration used by Ted Russell in "Football."

2. If you enjoyed this selection by Ted Russell, you will enjoy reading others in *Tales from Pigeon Inlet* and *The Chronicles of Uncle Mose.*

3. See the biographical note on Ted Russell at the end of "Babysittin' " on page 5.

* * *

Getting Ready To Enjoy A Song

Folk songs can be about almost anything. Often such a song will describe some great event, such as a shipwreck, a battle, or the death of a great person. Many folk songs are beautiful love songs, some of which recount a happy occasion, such as a marriage, while others tell of lost love and heartbreak. Other folk songs are light-hearted and were made up for amusement and entertainment, or to poke fun at some person.

"Harbour Le Cou" describes a series of incidents in which a man (the singer) does something which he shouldn't do and gets properly paid for it. The story is told in a light-hearted fashion, and we get the impression that no great harm is done to anyone. As with most folk songs, there are several versions of "Harbour Le Cou," but they all tell the same story.

This is one of the more popular Newfoundland folk songs. Harbour Le Cou, although just a small community, is perhaps one of the best-known place names in Newfoundland. Many people, though, believe that it is an imaginary place. The name is used by mummers in identifying their place of origin to further confuse their hosts: Question — "Where do you come from, mummers?" Answer — "We comes from Harbour Le Cou!"

Harbour Le Cou

O boldly I asked her to walk on the sand,
She smiled like an angel and held out her hand;
So I buttoned me guernsey* and hove way me chew,
In the dark rolling waters of Harbour Le Cou.

My ship she lay anchored far out on the tide,
As I strolled along with this maid at my side;
I told her I loved her she said, "I'll be true,"
As I winked at the moon over Harbour Le Cou.

As we walked on the sands at the close of the day,
I thought of my wife who was home in Torbay;
I knew that she'd kill me if she only knew,
I was courting a lassie in Harbour Le Cou.

As we passed a log cabin that stood on the shore,
I met an old comrade I'd sailed with before.
He treated me kindly, saying, "Jack, how are you?
It's seldom I see you in Harbour Le Cou."

And as I was parting, this maiden in tow,
He broke up my party with one single blow,
Saying "Regards to your missus and wee kiddies two,
I remember her well, she's from Harbour Le Cou."

I looked at this damsel a-standing 'long side,
Her jaw it did drop and her mouth opened wide;
And then like a she-cat upon me she flew,
And I fled from the furies of Harbour Le Cou."

Come all you young sailors who walk on the shore,
Beware of old comrades you've sailed with before;
Beware of the maiden with bonnet of blue,
And the pretty young damsels of Harbour Le Cou.

Traditional

Understanding What You Have Read

1. Rewrite in common everyday English the following colourful expressions:

   a) I chanced to espy
   b) Her place of abode
   c) I buttoned me guernsey
   d) ...hove way me chew
   e) ...this maiden in tow
   f) I fled from the furies

2. Is there an indication that Jack is just a little stupid to be "courting a lassie in Harbour Le Cou?"

3. Contrast the attitudes of Jack and the girl to the existence of the "missus and wee kiddies two."

4. What do you think of what the "old comrade" did? Was it intentional?

Things To Do

1. Try to think of at least one folk song for each of the following categories:

   a) Describing a great event
   b) Describing the death of a great person
   c) About a supernatural happening
   d) Concerned with love and heartbreak
   e) Giving an account of an organization or series of events
   f) Humorous songs

2. Find Harbour Le Cou and Torbay on a map of the island of Newfoundland.

3. Do the place names suggest anything about Newfoundland history?

4. Can you find out what Harbour Le Cou means?

5. Enjoy the song by singing it, or by listening to it being sung. Do the same for some of the songs you listed for question one.

6. Sketch any one of the scenes described in the song.

* * *

Jim Winter

Jim Winter

A CHANGING COUNTRY

Changes can be thought of as ideas — ideas which create new machines, new styles, new ways of life. Change leads to different behaviour and beliefs.

During the past thirty years social and technological changes have affected Newfoundlanders and their values as you will read in "Profit and Loss" and "Those New Ideas". They set people against people as is shown in "Tom Cods", "Night School" and "District Nurse". And in new ways change caused the loss of a community as in "Stage" and the waste of a fine ship described in "*S.S. Cabot Strait*". But on the more humorous side, change means laughter in Ted Russell's "District Nurse" and Art Scammell's "Night School". In a changing country we must watch the balance between things gained and things lost.

Getting Ready To Read

"Things aren't the way they used to be." "My, how times have changed." Those expressions you hear often, spoken by the old people who have lived and seen all kinds of new ideas brought into action. And really there has been no other period in Newfoundland history more full of changes than the nineteen fifties, sixties, and seventies. But the truth that's often missed with regard to change is that most new ideas replace old ones; that with changes, many good and valuable things are lost. This is the theme (main idea or thought) running through "Those New Ideas." The speaker, Uncle Mose of Pigeon Inlet, is concerned that the new ideas coming to Pigeon Inlet are changing Pigeon Inlet for the worse. Yet, by the end of the essay, you will be surprised to learn that Uncle Mose doesn't "practice what he...."

Those New Ideas

If a man had nothin' else to do only hang around Levi Bartle's shop and keep his ears cocked, he'd learn enough in a week to write a book. And what Levi Bartle could tell if he was so minded! But of course Levi don't tell anything because he might lose business by it.

One day last spring I was standin' up by Levi's counter waitin' my turn to get served, waitin' that is until Emma Jane Bartle was finished doin' her shoppin', and I couldn't help overhearin' what was said. Emma Jane wanted a pound of butter, and she was in an awful state because Levi didn't have the kind she wanted. Oh, he had two or three kinds like he's always got, but for a spell I figgered Luke Bartle'd have dry bread for his supper that night. Finally she took a pound of the old fashioned kind and went off. I asked Levi what 'twas all about and he told me how Emma Jane wanted the special kind she'd been hearin' about lately over the radio. I asked him what was special about it, was it any better or cheaper, and he said no. But 'twas already cut up in quarter pound blocks — four small blocks in every pound package — and Emma Jane thought there was a big advantage in havin' a pound of butter cut in four without her havin' the trouble of cuttin' it herself.

Now, as everyone knows, except probably Emma Jane herself, she's got peculiar notions, and for a while I thought no more about it. But later on I got to thinkin' and wonderin' where in the world is it goin' to end. 'Twould be laughable if it wasn't so serious. Take this kind of toothpaste they're advertisin' nowadays. Skipper Joe was in the house with me the night we first heard about it over the radio and I thought he'd kill hisself laughin'. It seems 'tis a wonderful improvement over the old kinds 'cause you don't even have to squeeze the tube to get at the paste. You get it out by what they call push button action and all you've got to give it is a feather touch instead of havin' to strain your muscles, or risk bustin' a blood vessel by squeezin' the tube. I asked Skipper Joe what he was laughin' at and he wiped his eyes and said he was thinkin' what a blessin' 'twould have been if they'd had that kind of toothpaste aboard the schooner in the days when he used to go to Labrador. Just think he said, of all the time and effort that would have been saved by men like Uncle Sol Noddy and Skipper Lige Bartle if they'd had push button feather touch toothpaste instead of a kind you actually had to squeeze out.

But jokin' aside, where's it goin' to end? And how many servants do we poor people think we can afford to have workin' for us, cuttin' up our butter and riggin' up toothpaste so that 'twill come out with a feather touch? The only thing that saves us down here is that we're so far behind the times. We still do old fashioned things like cuttin' up our own 'baccy instead of buyin' it already cut up for us, and our women bake their own bread instead of payin' someone to bake it for 'em. And Jake Briggs who's not long back from St. John's says that in there people won't buy bread any more unless it's sliced for them too. Think of all the work saved by not havin' to slice your own bread.

Grandma says there's no sense any more in tryin' to bake a cake. She used to be the champion cake baker in Pigeon Inlet, but now you can buy the cake already in a box and all you've got to do is stir it up, put an egg with it and bake it. Now Soos Noddy can bake just as good a cake as Grandma. That's all right in its way but there's no longer any reason for a woman to take pride in her work.

What disturbs me is the thought that if we want all this in the products we buy, is it any wonder we're havin' so much trouble with the products we're tryin' to sell. If I want (which I don't, but Emma Jane does) a pound of butter wrapped up in four quarter pound lots, why shouldn't the woman in the West Indies want her salt codfish done up the same way. And here are we tryin' to sell it to them in four quintal cakes. And tryin' to sell herrin' in barrels instead of glass jars.

'Tis all very wonderful, even the parts of it we've got down here in Pigeon Inlet. For instance it's years since I've used my molasses keg, for molasses, that is, 'cause I get my molasses at a lot higher price in what they call handy convenient tin cans. I don't even have to strain my arm ladlin' out a spoonful of sugar. All I've got to do is tip up the patent sugar dish Aunt Sophy gave me for Christmas and exactly one spoonful comes out at a time.

Grampa Walcott says that all these fancy ways of savin' labour are just fads got up to please the women 'cause they know if they can get the women foolish enough to buy 'em the men'll have to pay for 'em. All it's really doin' is addin' on to the cost of livin' and makin' it harder and harder for us to get by. Grampa says we men ought to put our foot down and stop it and I agree with him. But my kettle is singin' on the kitchen stove and I must make myself a cup of tea. Now where's that pound of tea I bought today from Levi Bartle? Yes, here it is. What? Loose tea! The nerve of Levi Bartle givin' me loose tea when he knows well enough I want tea bags. Why should I have a mess of tea leaves floatin' around in my cup? I've just got time to take it back to Levi's shop before he closes and make him change it. And that's exactly what I'll do.

Ted Russell

Understanding What You Have Read

1. a) Why was Emma Jane all upset with Levi Bartle?
   b) Do you think she was justified in being all upset? Are many people you know like Emma Jane in that way?

2. a) Explain how the new kind of toothpaste was a silly idea.

b) What modern conveniences do we have that may be seen as silly ideas?

3. What old-fashioned things have not yet disappeared in Pigeon Inlet? Have they disappeared in your community?

4. a) What did women such as Grandma Walcott lose by the introduction of the new cake mix?
   b) What are the disadvantages and results of all "those new ideas"?

Things To Do

1. Look around you. What changes have occurred in your homes, school, church and community in your lifetime? What was gained? What was lost?

2. See the biographical note on Ted Russell at the end of "Babysittin' " on page 5.

* * *

Justin Hall

Getting Ready To Read

Arthur Scammell for his short story "Night School" returns to the home of his birth and childhood, Change Islands. His characters are the unlikeliest students you could meet: Uncle Neddie, Tom Dowell, and Henry Parker. Each one of them is a hard-nosed, crusty fisherman: independent and proud, and eager to catch the eye of a pretty woman. The pretty woman happens to be the new school teacher. So to learn readin', 'ritin', and 'rithmetic, and to impress the pretty young teacher, the three salty fishermen try out a new idea: night school.

As you read "Night School" you will notice that the speaker in the story is Uncle Neddie, an old Change Islands fisherman, who tells the story using the words, phrases, and expressions commonly spoken in the area in which he lives. We say the story is written in dialect. To write a story in dialect is a very difficult task, because it requires three skills: a vivid memory, a keen ear, and sharp writing skills. Arthur Scammell demonstrates his possession of these skills. As you read try to hear Uncle Neddie's dialect as he tells the story of "Night School."

Night School

Uncle Neddie leaned back in his flour-barrel chair, lit his pipe and expatiated* on his favourite subject: Heducation is like good hearty grub. Some people it hurts, some thrives on it. It all depends on their constitootion.*

Last winter, for instance, we had a night school teacher come around to teach folks what was a little behind on their larnin'. Trim little craft she was too. Lines on her like a Nova Scotia banker. A few days after she come ashore in the mailboat, I was talkin' to Tom Dowell an' Henry Parker.

"Well, Neddie," ses Tom, winkin' at Henry, "I s'pose you'll be trottin' off to night school the winter."

"Yes," I said, surprisin' 'em. "I don't know but I will. I knocked off school at the 'Loss of the Royal Jarge,' in the number four Reader. There's lots of things I'd like to brush up on." Hearin' that kind of took the wind out of their sails.

"You ought to come along too, b'yes," ses I. "After all, you haven't got much to do this winter, clear of knittin' some twine an' gettin' a bit o' wood."

That started 'em thinkin', and the result was that when school opened the first night, there was Tom and Henry with a brand-new scribbler apiece, all washed up an' combed to beat the band. Pretty Miss Nicholls, the teacher, had 'em right under her thumb from the start.

"Mr. Dowell," ses she, when school closed the first night, "will you take the fire for the first week?"

Callin' him mister an' smilin' at him like that made Tom grin all over. No wonder it might, poor chap. Tom's wife had a different name for him an' she never axed* him to do something. She told him.

"Sartinly, miss," Tom answers. "I'll have that old bogey* sweatin' blood."

She had plenty of patience an' determination, an' if ever a girl earned her money that one did. It took her the best part of a week to teach Henry that he'd larn to write faster if he didn't hold his pencil like a splittin' knife. When it came to 'rithmetic an' dismals (decimals she called 'em), Henry was better, but Tom was hopeless. He'd make great big ones and scatter 'em among the figgers anywhere at all. Try as she might she never got him to call 'em by their right names. He started in by callin' 'em cast-net balls, an' nothing would change him.

I went over to Tom's one night afterwards for a game of checkers. His missus met me at the door.

"Where's the skipper?" ses I, free and aisy-like.

"Doin' his 'omework," she ses. I could see right off she was in a bad mood. "He's been at it now for two hours an' he got me nigh foolish. Keeps on suckin' his pencil an' mutterin'. Go in and talk to him."

Tom was nearly in the horrors when I went in the kitchen. He was ravin' about prices an' merchants, tellin' 'em where they could go, and givin' 'em the exact directions for gettin' there.

"What's the matter?" I asked him when I got a chance.

"Look here," he ses, "you know them sums we had to do. A can of bakin' powder and three pounds of onions cost $65.00 Here's where I worked it out." He showed me a piece of brown wrappin' paper covered with what he called figgers.

"It's them cast-net balls again, Tom," I ses. "I bet you got 'em in the wrong place. Just like I thought. Now give that dismal another berth* over under the lee of that six, and anchor 'en fore and aft so he'll bide thar."

When his wife come in later she was in a better mood until Tom mentioned he had to get his kindlin' for next night's school. Then she broke out again.

"Them turns of dry wood is gettin' a cuttin'," she ses. "It's about time somebody else took the fire."

I motioned to Tom to let her bide and we sot down to checkers while his wife rocked away, knittin'. Every ten minutes she'd look up from the muffler she was doin' for him and make nasty remarks, like suggestin' that he go easy on the butter when he used it to get the balsam gum off his hands before goin' to school, and askin', sarcastic*, if he had a clean pocket-handkerchief, and whether Miss Nicholls looked to see if he washed behind his ears. Tom didn't say nothin' but the fierce look in his eyes made me give him two games before I thought 'twas safe to try for a king.

Henry's wife wasn't very enthusiastic about night school either. Specially after she woke up one night an' caught him talkin' about the teacher in his sleep, and wishin' he was twenty years younger. She wrote a note to Miss Nicholls the next mornin' tellin' her not to keep Henry after school, as he had to be in bed early on account of his rheumatiz.

Everything was goin' along in school number one. Tom and Henry was workin' their heads off tryin' to build up pints for prizes that Miss Nicholls told us would be given at the night school closin'.

Then something happened which made Tom and Henry forgit their rivalry for a while. The Ranger (that's our pleeceman) started to court Miss Nicholls. It was beginnin' to look serious. Tom and Henry didn't like it a bit. One night Tom missed school on account of a cold he got gettin' his feet wet breakin' the path through the snow for the teacher the night before. Henry didn't go either when he heard Tom wouldn't be there. 'Twouldn't be fair he said. If he had more pints than Tom when school closed, Tom'd be throwin' that up to him. I went over to see Tom after school was out. Henry was there rubbin' Tom's chest with goose grease. Tom's wife was just leaving. "The night-school teacher give 'im the cold," she said, "and she can cure 'im."

"Look here, Neddie," says Tom, "me and Henry don't like Ranger courtin' Miss Nicholls. She's too good for him, eh Henry?"

"She sure is," Henry agreed. "I got no use for that dolled-up hangashore.* He's a city man an' he thinks he can boss everybody around here."

"I don't like him much more'n you two," I told 'em, "but I'm afraid the teacher do. She hurried the work through tonight because he was outside waitin' for her."

"There you are," ses Henry, disgusted, "just because this human mistake in a uniform rolls his eyes at her our heducation is goin' to suffer."

Tom stuck up for Miss Nicholls. "You can't blame her. I guess she's kinda lonely an' the Ranger seems to be able to get any girl he wants."

"Some of our own boys should be in there givin' him a run for his money," Henry said. "When I was a young feller if a girl like that come in the place, he'd be a smart outsider that 'ud get 'er."

"They've been tryin'," I answered, "but I guess they got discouraged, specially when the Ranger got to winnard* of 'em."

"What they wants is a little pushin'," suggested Tom. "I'm goin' to get after Jim Humphreys. Jim ought to be able to cut that Ranger out."

"I'll have a talk to Walter Murphy," offered Henry. "Walter's a good steady chap. Between the two of 'em they ought to make things interestin'."

Competition in the courtin' of Miss Nicholls picked up quite a bit after that. Tom and Henry done a good job on Jim and Walter. In a way, I sort of pitied the Ranger. Every night after school Jim and Walter'd be there waitin' to see her home. The Ranger turned up the first night, but the boys took his long, leather boots off and hinted to him that Miss Nicholls wouldn't like being 'scorted home by a man in his stocking feet. The teacher missed him and didn't take very kindly to Jim's and Walter's attentions. But the Ranger was game. The next night he was prepared for 'em. When they tried to interfere with him he blacked Jim's right eye and broke Walter's jaw. Jim wore a piece of out-of-season moose meat on his eye for a week. That was the only way he could get back at the Ranger.

But now Henry and Tom had to think up another plan. Miss Nicholls gave us all a composition to write just after that. We could choose any subject to write on and the both of them wrote on "Why I don't like Rangers." They had two weeks to write it in and, of course, they wanted me to help 'em, lookin' up the words in the dictionary and spellin' 'em out. I was never much of a hand at writin' and before them compositions was done I was sorry I ever agreed to be mixed up in it. Henry'd get some ideas during the day on why he didn't like Rangers and when he'd tell us about it at night Tom'd argue that he'd thought about the same thing and wanted it for his composition. They'd start rowin' then and I'd have to step in and get 'em to share up the pints they wanted to get down. I never saw men work so hard as Tom and Henry did over them essays. When they'd get excited over something they was puttin' down they'd press so hard their pen-nibs'd just cut through the paper or crumple up like a piece of rabbit wire. Night after night I coaxed 'em to give it up and try some easier plan, but they wouldn't hear of it. The writin' fever was in their blood and they couldn't stop.

The second week the both of 'em, Tom and Henry, got caught by the Ranger with a brace of partridge apiece in closed season. They had to pay a fine. After that I didn't go over to help 'em with their compositions. The words they'd have wanted me to spell wouldn't have been in the dictionary anyway.

The night we had to pass in our compositions Henry wasn't at school. I saw Tom pass in his and asked him where Henry was.

Tom shook his head.

"Henry," he said sorrowfully, "is not hisself nor won't be for a day or so. When he went to look for his composition tonight before comin' to school he couldn't find it. Hunted high and low he did. He asked his wife about it and found she cleaned the lamp chimney with it by mistake and then hove it in the stove. She was goin' to get the Ranger to him he carried on so, but I persuaded her not to. That's what made me late."

Next school night Miss Nicholls kept me and Tom behind after the others left. She came over to where we was sittin' and looked at us with her appealin' blue eyes.

"Mr. Dowell," she said, low and soft-like, "you and I have always been good friends, haven't we?"

"Sure we 'ave," agreed Tom.

"I'm glad to hear you say so," Miss Nicholls continued, "but that composition you did for me hurt me, oh, so much." She put 'er 'and to 'er 'art. "You know Ranger Thompson is another good friend of mine and I want my friends to like one another. I'm sure if you really knew him you'd like him, too, Mr. Dowell. He's so gentle and kind."

Tom was beginnin' to squirm in his seat. "I don't like Rangers anyway, Miss," he muttered. He was sort of ashamed to bring up about the little trouble he'd had with the law.

But why, Mr. Dowell?" She was standin' right beside Tom now with her 'and on 'is shoulder. "The reasons you gave in your composition were not reasons at all. They were only prejudices. We must be fair, you know, in our judgment of others. A Ranger has his job to do and he must do it without fear or favour." She turned to me. "Mr Baker here, I'm sure as an educated man agrees with me, don't you Mr. Baker?"

Well, she had me, round as a hoop. I wanted to help Tom but how could I? I could see she really was in love with Thompson and you can't argue with a woman in love. Besides, what she was sayin' was sensible, when you come to think it over.

"I think Miss Nicholls is right, Tom," I stammered helpless.

"I knew you two would see it my way," she smiled at us, her eyes shinin'. She was pattin' Tom's hand now in 'er gladness an' I knew that she was convertin' him twice as much as what she was sayin'.

"Now, I'm going to tell you a secret for bein' such good boys." She had 'er hands clasped now an' her eyes was like the stars outside. "The Ranger and I are engaged. Isn't it wonderful?"

Tom and I muttered congratulations an' stumbled out. We didn't say nothin' until we reached my house. Then Tom spoke.

"They'll make a fine couple," he choked. "Ranger Thompson's all right."

Them blue eyes an' the rest of it had done their work. I didn't blame 'im. But I wondered what Henry was goin' to say.

Henry said plenty an' he said it often. He couldn't understand Tom's change over. You couldn't expect 'im to, of course. He hadn't been kept in after school like me and Tom. We done what we could with him, to get him to like the Ranger, but 'twasn't much use. Tom even tried pattin' his 'and like Miss Nicholls, but it only lead to a lot o' bad language from Henry.

The last month of night school they was competin' agin' one another something fierce, tryin' to win prizes at the closin'. Their nerves was all shot to pieces, stayin' up studyin', an' every time they'd meet, they'd row reglar. At last school was over and they both got one prize each for good conduct. Miss Nicholls left.

"Hello Tom," ses Zeke Brake, one Saturday night as Tom entered his shop. "You're lookin' a bit white around the gills. Night school took it out of you, eh?"

"You can't get an heducation without workin' for it," answers Tom, in a tired voice.

Arthur Scammell

Mr. Arthur Scammell was born on Change Island and spent his early years there, near the squid jigging ground about which he wrote his famous song. He was educated at Change Islands and St. John's before moving to Montreal where he taught school for over twenty years. He finished his teaching career on the faculty of Memorial University's English Department.

Mr. Scammell has written for various publications, and co-founded the regional periodical **The Atlantic Guardian.** *His writing includes songs, ballads, poems, essays and short stories.*

He is a frequent guest speaker around the province, and a

welcome guest in many high school English classes. Mr. Scammell and his wife now reside in St. John's.

Understanding What You Have Read

1. Why does Uncle Neddie decide to go back to school? What was Tom's and Henry's reason?

2. How was Miss Nicholls different from Tom's wife?

3. Why was Henry's wife "not enthusiastic" about Tom attending night school?

4. What reason do Tom and Henry give for objecting to the Ranger courting Miss Nicholls? What is the real reason?

5. Why did the Jim-and-Walter plan to break up Miss Nicholls and the Ranger fail?

6. Miss Nicholls told Tom that the reasons he gave in his composition for not liking the Ranger were only prejudices. What did she mean?

7. What caused Tom to change his mind about the Ranger? Did Henry change his mind? Why or why not?

Things To Do

1. Scammell's use of dialect produces a humorous story. The use of certain phrases or expressions in certain conditions can be very funny. For instance, Tom calls decimals "cast-net balls." Uncle Neddie, in showing Tom how to multiply using decimals, says, "...now give that *dismal* another *berth* over *under the lee* of that six...." Quote examples of other words, phrases, or expressions, that make you smile.

2. Uncle Neddie loves to use very unusual similes. That is, he is continually comparing two different things by using the

words "like" or "as." For example, in the first paragraph of "Night School" he says " Heducation is like good hearty grub." Find and quote three other examples of similes.

3. "Night School" contains words which are unfamiliar or strange to you. A list of some of these words is below. Check the meanings of those words in the glossary.

expatiated
constitootion
axed
bogey
sarcastic
berth

* * *

Carol Crocker

Getting Ready To Read

Bernice Morgan chooses St. John's during the exciting days of World War II as the setting for her story "Profit and Loss." St. John's during the years 1939 to 1945 was all hustle and bustle because of the thousands of soldiers, airmen, and sailors, men and women, settling in or passing through the city. It was a time of over-night changes, a time when old ideas were replaced by newer ones. It was also the time when the Americans came to town, and nothing has ever been the same since.

Back then girls and boys had to learn quick lessons. You will see this is true of the speaker in "Profit and Loss." The Americans came into her life, changed it, and left. But their presence taught her a lesson of how money can be gone as quickly as it comes, but attitudes and viewpoints last for a life time.

Profit And Loss

When I was very young, men were men, children were children and a vacant lot was just that — a vacant lot. I know because we lived across the street from one. We called it "The Field." We dug holes in The Field, we made traps for our enemies and hiding places for our treasures. We crawled through the sky-high grass hunting tigers and tried to light fires with broken bottles. It was an aimless, empty, littered* place.

But that all changed, quickly with much rumbling and crashing of gears, all in one morning. A big yellow monster came grinding up and bit into the green sod, levelling and rolling smooth the brown earth — and before our eyes The Field disappeared and something new and altogether different took its place — a baseball diamond!

The Americans had arrived! They poured out of their khaki-coloured trucks into our field. With crew cut heads and tanned faces, dressed in white sweat shirts and blue jeans they raced about laughing and shouting, poking each other in the ribs, playing leap frog and behaving in a generally outlandish* manner. We were a silent and resentful little group as we stood there watching them, us girls in starched cotton dresses, our ribbed stockings wrinkled around our skinny legs, the boys in heavy tweed breeks* wearing white shirts and decent dark ties. These new creatures were just as big as our fathers but we had never seen our fathers act like this, the very thought turned us cold. Those oversize children had appropriated our field; the injustice of it overwhelmed us!

Then suddenly from out of the sunshine sticks of chewing gum rained down upon us and in one second all of our resentment vanished and we capitulated.* We did not know it then but also in that second the entire economy of our little world flipped over and nothing was ever the same again.

Today it is quite popular to dislike Americans, especially Americans outside their own country, but how kind those Americans were to us — and how we loved them. They came to the field (now the baseball diamond) every day, they taught us to play baseball and to use American slang. To me at least they all looked just alike, I could never tell one from another, any of them would respond to one of three names — Chuck, Mac or Joe.

It took us innocent, unspoiled natives about one hour to realize the commercial possibilities of the situation. It began quite innocently, midway through the first game of the afternoon my brother Tom ran home and returned with a glass and a jug of ice-water. Quite unexpectedly nickels and dimes were pressed into his palm, soon his breek pockets rattled with American coins.

If mere water brought Tom such a fabulous display of wealth — what would soft drinks do! We held a conference, everyone except Tom emptied their pockets, we had six cents between the four of us — very small capitalization* even in those days! But when Tom counted his loot we discovered he had fifty-six cents. Just think of it, fifty-six cents for one jug of ice water! After much persuasion, "If you don't I'll tell who broke the basement window" and some bargaining, "I'll give you me lucky alley and a stick of gum," we convinced the reluctant entrepreneur* to invest in the common fund. Then we all set off to the nearest store for soft drinks, that we called beer, and we were in business!

The profit was unbelievable and it was inevitable* that we should attract competition. A rival group of urchins from the other side of the field arrived and were soon doing as good a business as ourselves. We took a good long look at our rivals and decided that strong-arm methods would not work. They were all bigger than us and looked a good deal tougher. Besides, when Tom took a menacing step towards the smallest the young squirt informed us with a leer that his father was a policeman. This was a time-honoured ruse*, we had often used it ourselves. Still, who knew? It just might be true. As Tom said, it was no good looking for trouble.

We would have to depend on brains and know-how to outwit them, after all we'd been in business longer than they! So we got Tom's wooden hand-cart to speed up our trips to the store. We had noticed that the Americans showed a strong preference for Coke — our rivals stuck to our own favourite "Root Beer," and so by fast delivery and shrewd buying we got the better of them.

When, at sunset, we swaggered home, each of us was a millionaire. Of course our mother insisted that we pay for a broken jug and Tom was adamant* in his demand that the refunds on empty bottles were to be his alone. Rolling in our new-found wealth we could not find it in our hearts to be mean. We even gave our baby brother ten cents! The poor child was too small to cross the street.

It was a glorious summer. Never had any child of our acquaintance had so much cash. Mrs. Lane's tiny bulls-eye shop on the corner prospered greatly. Mrs. Lane put in daily stocks of Mary-Janes and jelly beans, supply could barely keep up with demand and our mothers noticed that Mrs. Lane had a new chesterfield and was getting her hair set every week.

Our parents were sure we would all be ruined — I heard my father tell a neighbour that he was seriously considering giving up work and letting us support him. They tried to channel some of our earnings into savings. "Why don't you buy some of these pretty war savings stamps, see how you can lick them and stick them onto the little squares?" but we would not be lured into any such traps. We were the 'nouveau riche.' No hidden store of wealth for us, the rage to spend was on us and we could not race to the corner store fast enough. The sky was the limit, marshmallow snow balls and double decker ice-cream cones were the order of the day. For years afterwards every stomach pain and dental cavity was attributed* to "that summer you stuffed yourselves with American money."

After every boom there must come a recession and ours came in late July. The Americans had finished a large baseball diamond on the Base itself — they would not be using our field again.

That first morning we waited and they didn't come. We were incredulous — surely they would come. We waited and waited, our 'beer' got warmer and warmer. Finally we sat down and drained our stock. Maybe they would come tomorrow — but they didn't. Grass began to grow into the diamond again, and again we were broke. We did not accept our new poverty philosophically* but grumbled and groaned among ourselves. It is very hard to reduce one's standard of living! Bitterly we thought of the dozens of chocolate bars and ice cream cones we'd consumed.*

Our parents' sympathy was not unmixed with many, 'I told you so's.' Only Mrs. Lane appreciated how we felt.

It would be nice to be able to say that we all learned such a thorough lesson in economics that we grew to be conservative yet astute* businessmen, that thanks to our early training we cleaned up on the stock market. Such is not the case. We are still, I am afraid, among the crickets of this world — just as broke as our neighbours. However what we do retain from that distant, bountiful summer is a fond regard for Americans, who, in our memory, are a nation of sunburned child-men frolicking in our field and channeling gold into our pockets.

Bernice Morgan

Born and raised in St. John's, Bernice Morgan has written many essays, short stories and plays set in St. John's and inspired by the people and events that made up her early life. She has received provincial recognition in having several of her plays produced by CBC, and national consideration in magazines such as **Newscene.** *As a member of a panel of three she edited* **From This Place**, *a selection of writing by women of Newfoundland and Labrador. Her home is still St. John's, where she works as communications officer with the Newfoundland Teachers' Association.*

Understanding What You Have Read

1. a) Why did the Americans come to "The Field?"
   b) What kind of men were they? What particular quality did the Americans possess that impressed the children?

2. a) How did Bernice and her friends make a profit from the Americans?
   b) What does she mean when she says, "...supply could barely keep up with demand"?
3. What did the children do with all their easily-earned money?

4. What is meant in the story by the phrase "After every boom there must come a recession"?

5. The money the writer earned she spent, but she kept something perhaps more valuable. What was it she kept?

Things To Do

1. Bernice Morgan makes use of a very broad vocabulary. Listed below are some of the words used in "Profit and Loss." Check their meanings in the glossary or a dictionary — then chose any five and discuss in class various ways they may be used.

vacant	'nouveau riche'
capitulated	philosophically
capitalization	astute
adamant	resentful
incredulous	breek
outlandish	menacing
commercial	attributed
entrepreneur	consumed

* * *

Getting Ready To Read

This excerpt is taken from *Tom Cods, Kids and Confederation* by Tom Moore.

The scene which the author describes certainly would be typical of the late 1930s, 1940s and early 1950s in Newfoundland. The attitudes and viewpoints are also typical of those held by young children at that time.

Because of the characterizations given — how the people act, speak, dress and so on — we can visualize 'Fleet', Sydney, Betty-Ann, Billy Banks and others. If you pay careful attention to the details, you will feel as though you were a participant in the scene described.

Tom Cods

I remember when I was a boy in Newfoundland everyone called me 'Fleet'. My real name was John Russell Junior but I was always the one most excited when the fleet of American fishing boats came into our harbour every July for bait. I would run down the unpaved road at Petley and shout to my friends and neighbours "the fleet! the fleet!"

Our little harbour would be full of these schooners that fished for cod on the Grand Banks of Newfoundland. Because they fished the Banks they were called Bankers by everyone except me. Their sails of thick white canvas floated on the summer wind and those hearty American seamen waved to those of us who were on shore. We recognized many of them from previous voyages. Skipper Neddy Shay from Boston was the one with the cork leg. He would sit on the wharf while the crew were loading bait and cut off a piece of chewing tobacco with his long pointed splitting knife. Then if anyone was watching him he would finish by sticking the knife into his cork leg as he put away the tobacco. He always caught a few people with that trick every summer.

My favourite was Billy Banker who was Captain of the *Yankee Trader,* one of the biggest boats in the fleet. Billy Banker was the biggest and strongest of all those seamen who came to Petley. He had a thick red beard and always wore a red stocking cap on his head even on the hottest days in August.

Betty-Ann Martin said it was because he was bald.

Billy Banker sailed the *Yankee Trader* from Boston to New York during the spring carrying Boston fish to the New York market. He used to tell us stories about the people of New York and how they lived in that big city. He told us about motor cars, and air planes and the clothes the people wore and what they did. Betty-Ann said that it was a pack of lies, and even some of the boys thought that he told a few stretchers, but I believed every word that Billy Banker said. I knew that he was a man who would not tell a lie. Just to watch Billy bring the *Yankee Trader* in around the point and safely into Petley harbour a good half hour ahead of any of the other boats, to watch his beaming crew throw out their anchors and row smartly ashore, to watch Billy Banker standing in the bow while all hands rowed,and to watch him jump smartly upon Petley wharf, the first man ashore, you knew right away that he was a man who didn't need to lie or tell stretchers.

The fleet stayed ashore as they waited for enough bait fish to fill their boats. This was usually a week, for according to the law in Newfoundland the Americans were not allowed to catch the bait themselves, but had to buy it from the local fishermen. This worked out to everybody's advantage as there were lots of men in Petley who caught the bait fish like caplin and squid and sold it to the Americans.

During that week the American fishermen would spend their days mending their nets and preparing for their trip to the Grand Banks, the home of the cod fish. They would stroll around the few unpaved streets of Petley, buy supplies at the only store, and renew old acquaintances in the town. Boys my own age, free from the confines* of school, would spend our days down on the wharf fishing for tom cods and listening to the Americans. You could just sit and listen to them for hours. They were full of interesting stories and they spoke quite differently from us. They spoke slower and clearer with a drawling accent that you could recognize anywhere. Wally Martin, also my cousin, used to mimic* them really well when he was out of ear shot of the wharf.

In the evenings our own fishermen would come in from the jigging grounds with boat loads of squid to sell to the

Americans. Then the wharf was all a'bustle as the squid was being unloaded and weighed and the Petley fishermen were paid for their catches in cash. Ready cash was a rare commodity* in those days. Jokes were exchanged by the men and stories told about the day's fishing. Some of these jokes were not meant for our young ears and I will not repeat them here, but we heard them just the same and pretended not to listen or to understand. Wally Martin would go and tell them to all the girls the first chance he got.

A gang of kids around my own age used to gather under the land end of the wharf in the afternoon when the tide was out. This was when Wally Martin and Sydney Clouter would tell their stupid jokes and stories hoping to impress the girls. Sydney was the minister's son who had just moved to Petley from Clarenville. He was worse than the rest. Sydney was telling a joke one afternoon when I was just coming off the wharf with my pole in my hand and a few tom cods on a string to bring home to the cat. I heard himself and Wally burst into gales of laughter when Betty-Ann said, "That's not funny at all Sydney Clouter. That's very foul and I've got a good mind to tell your father."

This last comment struck home and silenced our new comedian. Then she saw me and added, "You don't hear John Martin telling foul jokes like that." She never called me Fleet and I have since come to suspect that she had romantic designs on me. To tell the truth I always fancied that she was my girl for her patronage* and attentions gave me a great deal of prestige* with the gang.

Sydney was glad that the conversation had shifted from her telling his father the minister and he now turned to me. "No, Fleet is too good to tell stories like that. After all his father is from Canada." He said this last word with a contempt* that I had never before heard. True, Father was from Toronto, Ontario, but we never held it against him, since he had been living in Petley for the past eleven years. Sydney had already sensed my favour with Betty-Ann and a clash between the two of us was bound to occur. He was a year older than I was and I had seen him during the past few weeks trying to get the attention of Betty-Ann. He would jump from the wharf into a boat tied off and jump back again before anyone caught him at it. He would push around the younger boys and tell them that they'd better watch out or he'd do worse. In fact he sent many a lad home crying to his mother. No one could say a word about him because his father was the minister.

Now people called me "Fleet" but no one called me stupid, and I had been giving the matter some thought as I had been fishing on the wharf. I had come to the conclusion that sooner or later I was going to be forced into having it out with the upstart* Sydney.

So when he glared right at me and added, "People from Canada are too good for stories like that," there was no question in my mind as to what he meant. He meant trouble. I had seen fist fights before and most of them amounted to very little damage to either of the fighters. Boys my own age squabbled and scratched until some adult pulled them apart and sent them home with a kick in the pants. The men sometimes fought when they had been drinking at the parties that the Americans gave on the wharf. But these too were usually quite harmless and ended in a stream of unmanly oaths and curses from both fighters. Rather, I was going to style my fight on Billy Banker who knocked a big American face down on the wharf one summer. His style of fighting was to let the other fellow do all the talking and cursing, and as soon as he got within arms reach to poke him hard right in the mouth.

"Well look who's talking," Betty-Ann was picking up for me as best she could. "You're only moved here a month yourself smarty pants, so there."

"Can't the little darling say a word for himself," Sydney goaded*, and pushed me on the shoulder to make clear his challenge. I was about to land him a Billy Banker special in the mouth when I realized that I had a fishing pole in one hand and five tom cods in the other. I was rapidly trying to figure out which would be the worst across the face, a string of wet fish or a bamboo pole. He mistook this hesitation for fear and pushed his face up against mine. Unfortunately this was just when I had decided on the fish which were in my right hand. Out went my right arm in an arc aimed straight at his grinning face. Ahead went his grinning face, and my fish missed the mark and went along behind his head, around his neck, and back around my head, linking us together like two dancers. He was truly surprised by this sudden and unusual attack, as I was myself. The two of us fell together and jostled* on the slippery rocks, soon falling to the ground amid the shouts of our supporters and detractors.* We squirmed and slipped on the wet stones until he struggled to the top and sat on my stomach. My string of fish was still firmly strung around both our necks and I held tight to my end of the string with my right hand as the frustrated Sydney tried to break it. There I was temporarily saved from total defeat and disgrace by a string of wet fish. If that string broke and Sydney could sit on top of me, look down and say "There, I guess I showed you," then he wouldn't even have to push me. The fight would be over and he could get up and say "Come along Betty-Ann, let's go home." And I wouldn't blame her one bit if she turned up her nose at my lying there covered with defeat and tom cods, and go off with Sydney. That's how close I came. But such was not to be the case.

Amid the shouts and cheers a gruff but familiar voice boomed under the wharf. "What are you young ones doing down here?" There was silence. Sydney and I froze and hoped to go unnoticed. Two strong arms pulled us to our feet and a smart smack sent tom cods flying all around us. We both stood facing Billy Banker. "Now get home out of here all of you. You'd think a minister's son would have better sense," he concluded.

"Yes Mr. Banker, you would," Betty-Ann echoed pointedly. I was saved and joyfully gathered up my tom cods. Pole in hand, I marched up from under the wharf and strode off home. Sydney and Wally marched ahead sulking and no doubt plotting my doom. The rest followed with Betty-Ann and myself: Jimmy Winsor, Sue Winsor, Tony Martin, Billy Hubble. They all knew that I was no fighter, and they thought I was very fortunate to have escaped as well as I had. My fame among the gang rested in my being able to sit on the wharf and catch a tom cod when no one else could, and in having the favour of Betty-Ann who was a year or two older than the rest of us.

As I turned the corner of the fence to go in through our gate, I met Grandpa charging out and Father standing in the door. I then heard a name for the very first time that I was to hear thousands of times in the months to come. Grandpa turned his head and shouted back at Father, "Well I don't care if Joey Smallwood never comes. I hope they drown him down off the wharf." Now this was a curious remark, and why was Grandpa so angry?

"Who is Joey Smallwood, Father? And why is he coming to Petley?"

Father looked past me for a moment in the direction Grandpa had gone. Then, as if remembering my questions, he replied very seriously, "Joey Smallwood is the man who will save Newfoundland." That's all he said. Then he turned and went into the house.

This both interested and puzzled me. I did not know that we needed saving. Nor could I imagine from what. I had always been under the impression that Petley was the best of all places to live. True, we ate a lot of fish and potatoes but we were far from starving like the people over in Africa. In fact we used to send them church packages of food, wool mittens, and the like. Certainly I thought things were laid out very well in Petley. Some people had gone hungry during the depression or the "hard times" as the people called it, but the war had ended all that. Any young man who wanted a job had gone off to fight for king and country. Newfoundland was Britain's oldest colony and most of the men who fought joined the British navy. As well they should, Grandpa said.

Such were my thoughts as I went into our house in Petley that day. I was resolved to find out what was going on and decided to question my parents further on the matter.

Tom Moore

Tom Moore is a teacher and writer who has achieved recognition through the publication of his novel **Goodbye Momma.** *He has also published other prose in* **Kids, Tom Cods and Confederation,** *and poetry in* **Poems** *and in various magazines. A measure of international recognition is reflected in the publication of* **Goodbye Momma** *in translation in Denmark.*

Understanding What You Have Read

1. Read again the descriptions of Skipper Neddie Shay and Billy Banker. Close your eyes and picture each in your mind. Now write your own descriptions of each as you see them.

2. Fleet's father was from "Canada" and Sydney was the minister's son. Why would either of these conditions be sufficient to make the boys angry enough to fight. What attitude is illustrated?

3. What do you think of Betty-Ann? Support what you say by referring to specific incidents in the story. What attitude is illustrated?

Things To Do

1. At the end of the excerpt, we see the different attitudes towards Joey Smallwood at that time. Try to draw a conclusion as to why Fleet's father felt Joey was "the man who will save Newfoundland" and his grandfather hoped they would "drown him [Joey] down off the wharf."

   Discuss with your teachers the political situation of those times.

2. Read "Catching Conners" by Ray Guy and "Trout-Spearing" by Edward Wix in *Doryloads.*

3. Read Tom Moore's "The Caplin Scull" and "Ancestors" in *Baffles of Wind and Tide.*

4. Have a panel discussion. Compare the young people in this story with yourselves. How are you alike? How are you different?

* * *

Getting Ready To Read

Many Newfoundlanders have felt a deep sense of loss when resettlement programs and modern methods of fish processing have resulted in an abandonment of their small villages and traditional way of life. Read the following poem slowly. Then re-read it, stopping to reflect after each phrase you read.

When you see a series of dots as is used at the end of each stanza in this poem, you should know that the author wants you to pause — in this case, to continue thinking along lines similar to those he had indicated. If you do this, you will, undoubtedly, think of some other examples and be able to add your own lines to those already given by Tom Dawe.

Stage

No put put of the motor boat,
no waiting women placing boughs,
no children playing in the cliffs,
no cod-oil doors with painted moons,
no meadows green through caplin,
no sound-bone talk from tired men....

But one grey fish-stage
leaning seaward
from the cold sloping rocks
below the meadows
of the unmown hay....

Tom Dawe

Tom Dawe has won awards in the Newfoundland and Labrador Arts and Letters Competition for his short stories, poems, plays and sketches. This Newfoundland artist was born in 1940 at Long Pond, Manuels, in Conception Bay. He has had published numerous articles, poems, and stories, and has written extensively for radio. Collections of his poems have been published in **Hemlock Cove and After, In a Small Cove,** *and* **Connections.** *He is presently a member of the English faculty of Memorial University in St. John's.*

Understanding What You Have Read

1. The author describes a deserted scene. What words show that no one has been there for some time?

2. Describe in your own words, what is meant by: "women placing boughs", "cod-oil doors with painted moons", "meadows green through caplin", "sound-bone talk from tired men". (Remember that these people were 'fisher folk'.)

3. Try to place a value on what this author feels has been left behind when the 'stage' was abandoned.

Things To Do

1. The last stanza appeals to the artist in us. Sketch the scene described.

2. Look up the various dictionary entries for the word 'stage.' Could there be double or triple meanings to the title of this poem? If so, what are they? Discuss these with your teacher and classmates.

3. Try to visit a village where there are old-fashioned fishing stages still standing. Perhaps people no longer live there.

4. Do a little research on how fish was cured in years gone by — dried, salt bulk, etc.

* * *

Getting Ready To Read

Ted Russell has been known since the early 1950s in Newfoundland as a master story teller. Mr. Russell, as Uncle Mose, used humour to depict the lives and times of the people who live here.

For many years our province relied on district nurses who were stationed along the coast to provide medical care. They treated everyone — babies to grandparents — and every ailment. With few doctors and fewer hospitals the services of the district nurse were invaluable.

The District Nurse

Now I'm going to tell you how the District Nurse came to be stationed at Hartley's Harbour instead of here in Pigeon Inlet where she ought to be.

We wanted her here and Hartley's Harbour people were unreasonable enough to want her there. The government couldn't please everybody, so they told her to spend her second three months with us. Then she could decide for herself, and they'd build her dispensary* in whatever place she picked.

We in Pigeon Inlet figured out we couldn't lose — for three good reasons. First, a nurse'd want a nice clean store to do her shopping. We had that. Levi Bartle's store in Pigeon Inlet is away ahead of Lige Grimes' old place in Hartley's Harbour. Second, she'd want a good boarding house, and we had that. Aunt Sophy Watkinson's boarding house was famous all along the coast, while in Hartley's Harbour, she'd be lucky if she didn't starve to death at Aunt Sarah Skimple's. Third, and most important of all, she'd probably want some nice company her own age, and that was our strongest point. The Hartley's Harbour boys are all right in their own way, but not to be compared with young Lloyd Walcott, a handsome, strapping young fellow, just like myself thirty years ago. What more could a nurse want?

Well, in November she came down on the boat to Hartley's Harbour and we saw her on the deck of the steamer. Just out from England she was. Pretty little thing, but awful skinny. Anyway, if she didn't starve in the next three months, we'd fatten her up when we got her up in the Inlet in February. We were so sure of getting her now that we began to pick a place to build the dispensary.

We wouldn't have been so sure if we'd known that Lige Grimes had just given up chewing tobacco. He had cleaned up his store and put up a big notice. It read: NO SMOKING OR SPITTING ALLOWED. BY ORDER OF THE HARTLEY'S HARBOUR NURSE'S COMMITTEE. The hypocrite! But we didn't know that 'til 'twas too late.

At last one day in February the nurse moved in by dog team — bag and baggage — to start her three months with us. She looked thinner than ever, but Aunt Sophy was ready with a big supper for her and young Lloyd Walcott dropped in accidentally during the evening.

Our committee had a lot of meetings from then on and Grampa Walcott always had something good to report. Nurse's appetite was good and she was getting fatter every day. She liked Aunt Sophy and young Lloyd was up there every night. Grampa walked in on them in Aunt Sophy's room one night. He chuckled when he reported this to us and said that courtin' was the one thing that hadn't changed in the last sixty years.

In May the first steamer came and the nurse had to go back to St. John's. She said she'd have to report to the government before deciding where her headquarters would be, but we were sure we had her. Why, she looked a good thirty pounds heavier than she had three months ago. Levi Bartle even bet Lige Grimes a hundred dollars that we'd get her. I don't hold with bettin', especially with fellows like Lige Grimes.

Well, we got our shock a week later when me and Skipper Joe were sitting down in Levi Bartle's front room listening to the Gerald Doyle news bulletin. The bulletin was about three parts over when we heard this:

"Nurse Plumtree, who is in St. John's on official business, is returning by next boat to take up residence in her new headquarters at Hartley's Harbour."

We looked at each other. There must be some mistake. The bulletin continued: "Nurse Plumtree looks very fit and healthy after her winter in the North. She laughingly admitted to a reporter from this bulletin that she had put on much weight during the past three months, but that she intended to diet from now on till she had reduced to her normal weight."

We stared in amazement. What was he talking about? The bulletin continued: "Our Hartley's Harbour correspondent informs us that Mr. Lloyd Walcott of Pigeon Inlet has just accepted a position as bookkeeper with the enterprising firm of Elijah Grimes of Hartley's Harbour. Mr. Walcott will be taking up his new duties shortly."

I looked at Levi Bartle out of the corner of my eye. His face had turned white as a sheet.

The bulletin continued: "Mr. Grimes has just been awarded the contract to build the new nurse's dispensary in the up and coming town of Hartley's Harbour."

I looked again. Levi's face was turning from white to red — dark red. The reader continued: "The nurse's committee of Hartley's Harbour gratefully acknowledges receipt of a generous donation of one hundred dollars from Mr. Levi Bartle, a popular business man of the little settlement of Pigeon Inlet. This money will be spent by the committee for liquid refreshment at a time to be given in her honour when she arrives shortly to take up her permanent residence in Hartley's Harbour. It is expected that a good time will be had by all."

I looked again. Levi's face was purple now — a deep dark purple. Me and Skipper Joe Irwin tiptoed silently from the room and out through his back door.

You'd think that much of a victory would have satisfied the crowd from Hartley's Harbour. But no! They had to rub it in a bit harder. A few days later, Levi Bartle received something in a big flat envelope and wondered who was sending him a calendar in May. It was postmarked "Hartley's Harbour" and in one corner of the envelope was written: "You can hang this up in your store now — we're finished with it." Levi opened the envelope and found — yes, you've guessed it. It was a card-board notice showing signs of wear and tear. On it was written in big letters in indelible pencil: NO SMOKING OR SPITTING ALLOWED BY ORDER OF THE HARTLEY'S HARBOUR NURSE'S COMMITTE. Poor Levi was fit to be tied.

Well, that'll show you what we Pigeon Inlet people are going to be up against when we try to get a fish plant in Pigeon Inlet instead of in Hartley's Harbour. But we'll do it. Yes sir! You watch.

Ted Russell

Understanding What You Have Read

1. In your own words, tell briefly how Hartley's Harbour "got the best" of Pigeon Inlet.

2. In the days of this story to have some flesh (fat) on one's bones was greatly respected. What do you suppose thinness indicated? Why?

3. Notice how "Uncle" Mose calls people in the community "Skipper," "Aunt" and "Grampa." They are not especially his relatives. Why, then, would he refer to them in this way?

4. We find ourselves chuckling as we read this selection. Just what makes it humorous?

Things To Do

1. Listen to Ted Russell's record "The Chronicles of Uncle Mose."

2. Make up a yarn of your own. Tape record it. Let your friends and classmates hear it.

3. For excellent factual information on the early district nurses read *Don't Have Your Baby in the Dory*, a biography of Myra Bennett by H. Gordon Green and *Labrador Nurse* by B.J. Banfill.

* * *

Getting Ready to Read

Before 1965 and the completion of the Trans Canada Highway, Newfoundland depended largely upon its water routes for efficient transportation. Even today, our chief freight link with the mainland is to "cross the Gulf."

The coastal boats which plied our waters for so many years were a vital part of our lives bringing goods and people to our otherwise isolated communities.

For the people along the coast of Labrador these types of boats still play an important role.

The writer draws your attention to the fact that there are areas of our province where this type of transportation has become obsolete (no longer needed). The *S.S. Cabot Strait* spent many years making the crossing between Port aux Basques, Newfoundland, and North Sydney, Nova Scotia. Just before her "retirement" her route took her from St. John's along the northeast coast of Newfoundland and Labrador to Goose Bay and Nain. Note how the poem is written from the point of view of the steamer.

S.S. Cabot Strait

They say I'm too old.
They say I'm too slow.
They say I've outlived
my usefulness.
They say...
Wait
They say?
What do they know?
Nobody asked me.
After all
I should know
how old I am.
I can still remember
when I came down the ways

at Ferguson's.
Yes
that was in '47
Byes oh byes
I was some ship
"Queen of the Gulf"
they called me.
Yes my son
I remember
those were the times.

There was *Bar Haven*
Burgeo
Baccalieu
Springdale
and so many more.
I was there too
frolicking and dancing
up and down
the coast.
No, not me
I didn't pitch and roll
and wallow*
like these
foreign
slab-sided
floating box cars.
I had style and grace and...
and a Captain and a crew
one time
not now.

Not anymore.
They've chained me up now.
I wonder what they'll do
to me?

Maybe
I'll be sold foreign
like the *Leif,*
or scuttled*
like my sisters and cousins.
I'm waiting now
for the day
they haul me out
through the Narrows
the Notch, some call it.
On that day, do me a favour.
Go out to Fort Amherst
and
watch and wave
Good-bye.
Squint hard at me
that day
and if you see
salty tears
running down
my rusty hawse pipes
try to remember.
And
if you're too young
to remember
try to understand.

David Benson

David Benson is a poet whose work has appeared in the **Atlantic Advocate.**

Understanding What You Have Read

1. Why was the ship called "Queen of the Gulf"?

2. Why does the ship think she was different from the *Bar Haven* and others?

3. What does she think might happen to her?

4. At the end of the poem what favour does she ask of her readers?

Things To Do

1. Bring to school pictures of any of the old coastal boats. Show them to your classmates. Ask your parents or grandparents if they ever travelled on one of these boats. Tape record their experiences with this kind of travel and play the recording for the class.

2. Have a debate. Be it resolved that modern means of transportation are better than those of yesteryear.

3. The lounges on the coastal boats were great places for socializing. Read "Smokeroom on the *Kyle*" by Ted Russell in *Doryloads.*

4. Find out areas where the coastal boats still run. If you live in such an area describe the boat, or the scene when she docks, or a trip aboard her.

* * *

Justin Hall

Peter Ball

A LAND IN THE WEST ATLANTIC

Our province lies in the western part of a great ocean, buffeted by winds and tides, and often beset by blizzards and storms. One might think that our land is a barren and savage place. It has its winter frosts, but these are not without their own sparkling beauty, and it has spring mists and fogs, balmy breezes of summer and starlit nights of autumn. The land is covered with forests, meadows, lakes and rivers. Wildlife is abundant.

Thus while we do have our barrens, and we do have our wild places, Newfoundland is also a place of beautiful changing seasons on the land, the coastline and the sea.

Getting Ready to Read

"Newfoundland: The Winter Frosts" is a brief selection from Chapter One of *Life and Work in Newfoundland* by Reverend Julian Moreton.

As you read, ask yourself if the winters that the Reverend Moreton experienced are different from yours. Ask your grandparents or other older people if they can verify Reverend Moreton's accounts from stories *they* were told about the Newfoundland environment in the 1800s. Questions you must always ask yourself when reading any selection: Who is the speaker? What is his point of view? Is it slanted or objective? It is only in reaching answers to such questions that you will develop sound judgments on attitudes and opinions expressed by writers.

Newfoundland: The Winter Frosts

The severity of the winter frosts will best be appreciated from an account of some of its effects as I have experienced it.

All the ground freezes far below the surface, so that late in May when I began to dig my garden, the spade would turn up blocks of ice at a little more than half a spade's depth. This freezing of the earth uplifts the shores upon which the largest buildings rest, and thus the floors are thrown out of level, and often the doors cannot be closed until they have been hung afresh or otherwise altered. On very cold days the shrinking of all the timbers in wooden houses causes a succession of reports like the booming of heavy guns, often continued for several hours. I remember well the alarm I suffered when first I heard this in my own house. It was very late, and I was alone, with two or three hours' work in writing before me, which I was anxious to finish. Suddenly the dead silence of my room was broken by a heavy thump, as of a larger timber thrown against the wall before me. I got up and looked out. It was a splendid night. The moon shone brightly above, and the snow and ice spread everywhere below, making everything as visible as the day.

All was still, and almost awfully quiet. In those clear cold nights you conceive that if a pin dropt a hundred foot distant you must hear it. I returned within doors and resumed my writing, and at once the thump against the opposite wall was repeated; then one came by my side; two on the other side, or behind me; a volley; silence for a time, and then again one. I knew no cause for such sounds, and my nerves were so shaken I could write no more. I went to bed, but not to sleep, for the cannonade continued. At last, words recurred to my mind which a neighbour had used lately, that "on frosty nights the house would snap like guns". It was then, I knew, a natural effect of the frost which had thus disturbed me, and thankful for the recollection I sank to sleep.

Often the cold renders it almost impossible to sleep. Many such nights have I lain in more than semi-consciousness throughout; my feet aching; my nose positively smarting in spite, or perhaps in consequence, of frequent rubbings. Your breath congeals in a thin casing of ice upon your sheet and pillow, and upon any change of your position this dabs most uncomfortably upon your cheeks. A remedy which I sometimes used, and always found effectual, was to rise from bed and run two or three times with bare feet upon the still colder floor. This excites circulation, and soon a glow of warmth is felt which enables you to sleep.

When writing it was necessary for me to keep my ink glass constantly upon the hob* or in the fender*; and the ink in my pen would freeze so as to oblige me at every second line or oftener to hold it to thaw by the fire.

No kinds of food can be kept from frost, except in the cellars, which are built with earthern walls four feet in thickness. This, in a place like Greenspond where no butcher's meat could be bought in winter, was in one respect rather a convenience, for it was usual to get beef from St. John's by the latest vessel before winter, and hanging it in some store or outhouse, where it could continue nearly uniformly frozen, to cleave or saw off a joint as we wanted it. Meat and bone alike required the saw and hatchet.

The freezing of bread is as inconvenient as can be supposed, and many expedients are used to prevent it. The cellars are not suitable for this purpose because of their mouldy atmosphere. My first discovery of one very common mode of obviating this inconvenience was unpleasant enough. I was travelling to visit some of the many stations of my mission, and on my way stopped at a small island to hold divine service in a fisherman's house, for himself and his neighbours. After the service his mother asked me to take some tea before I went on my journey, and I gladly agreed to do so. While cutting bread and butter for me, my hostess complained of the difficulty of keeping the bread thawed, "and yet," she said, "I put the loaf in the bed, and wrap it up close as soon as ever the boys turn out." Alas for a weak stomach! However it was that food or none for me then, and I had to overcome all qualms. Little did I suspect that in my own house any such mode was used. One night, however, near the same time, my brother, who had lately come to me from England, wanted supper in my absence. The two servant girls were gone to bed, and upon searching the pantry himself he found no bread. In the morning plenty was on the breakfast table, and he asked how it was that none was to be found the night before. The girl's reply was, "O, sir, we always wrap up the bread and place it in the foot of our bed at night."

I believe it is a common practice of the fishermen's wives to keep their leaven* tied in a small bag in the bed all the winter.

Another circumstance which came under my notice will also serve to illustrate the extreme severity of the cold. There was in my parlour a brick-built closet, adjoining both the parlour and kitchen fire-places, and supposed to be warmed by them. In this closet was the wine for Holy Communion. One Sunday morning I looked there to see whether the wine was put out ready for use that day, and found it then in proper condition. An hour after, when I went to take it thence to the church, it was frozen as thick as fruit jelly, and could not be poured out.

Milk freezes solid, and we commonly cut it into pieces in the jug for use at the table.

If any coffee overflow your cup, it will quickly freeze in the saucer; so that upon raising the cup to drink its saucer is lifted with it.

The door-handles, fire-irons, and all other metal that you touch cling to your hand, and will tear off the skin if you too quickly relax your hold. The grasp must be continued till some warmth is communicated from your hand to the frozen metal.

The horses at work on the roads have icicles many inches long pendent from the hair in their nostrils; and something approaching to the same inconvenience often happens very unpleasantly, and even painfully, to human travellers.

The worst effect of the frost is frost-burning of the features, the limbs, or, as it sometimes happens the whole person. The last case is fatal. Few persons that live much out of doors in Newfoundland wholly escape this evil. A few moment's exposure sometimes suffices to produce a burn of slight character; as to myself, it has happened, my hands have been burnt in the brief act of tying my cap. My ears were many times burnt. In such a case the affected part soon recovers feeling, becomes tender for a day or two, then sheds the skin, and no mark is left. A schoolmaster at one of my stations had lost a great part of both hands and feet, owing to his being overtaken and outwearied in a storm. Aged people, having but languid circulation, are liable to frost burning in their beds. A very distressing case of this kind lately came under my own observation. It is not usual for people to travel alone, from fear of this burning. The affection is attended by no sensation informing the sufferer what has happened. Your nose perhaps, or another feature, becomes suddenly tallowy white. If you have a companion, he tells you your misfortune, and by proper means you restore circulation. But if no one sees the mischief, it proceeds , and soon after you recover warmth you lose the affected feature by sloughing*; and though nature after long suffering will skin over the maimed member, it will not restore the lost portion.

A frost-burn seems more difficult of healing than any other sore. My own infant child was for many years a sufferer in this way, though happily with no worse consequence than a scar on her foot. A few years ago, in the month of April, two men and two boys went out from Greenspond in a punt to shoot birds and seals. The drift-ice was then floating near the shore. An offshore breeze in the evening kept these poor men out, and drove them away with the ice. One of the men, who was aged, and the two boys after a time sank exhausted and benumbed to sleep, and in sleep their spirits passed away. Their companion, upon awakening, discovered that they were dead. He kept his energy better, and when, after (I think) three days' and nights' exposure, he was near succumbing, he had the good fortune to see a sleeping seal, which he managed to reach and kill. He sucked its warm blood and was reinvigorated. For a week he remained out in horrible loneliness, keeping his punt under the lee of the ice for shelter from sea and wind. At the end of that time a vessel picked him up and carried him to St. John's. His feet were burnt, and he suffered long and severely, till a surgeon cut them both off near the instep. He still lives, and walks and works with much less inconvenience than would be supposed.

A crew of eight men, wrecked in an English vessel by meeting a strip of ice near the Newfoundland coast, were brought to Greenspond in 1852 after eight days' exposure. All were burnt, and six of them had to lose limbs or parts of limbs. I was engaged in assisting the doctor in operating upon the worst sufferer, who had to lose by the knife all his fingers, one thumb, and both his legs.

Frost then, as well as many other circumstances of life in Newfoundland, is sufficiently disagreeable. Yet young and healthy men, fond of work and eager for adventure, will not complain of a few years spent in such a country. Most men know the pleasure of voluntarily enduring hardship and braving danger, and they who in such a spirit come to Newfoundland find positive enjoyment for a time. Sportsmen and men of science visit the country, and in their respective pursuits necessarily bear rough living and face danger, and are far from complaining of it afterwards. The minister of Christ in such a field has, all men know, much more to impel* and to sustain him; and may hope, when he retires, to have a far more delightful reward.

Reverend Julian Moreton

Reverend Julian Moreton, as a missionary for the Society for the Propagation of the Gospel in Foreign Parts, came from England to Greenspond; he served the widespread Greenspond Mission until 1850. Then he returned to England where he wrote an account of his eleven years of missionary work in Bonavista Bay called **Life and Work in Newfoundland.** *Moreton's Harbour is named after this 19th century English missionary.*

Understanding What You Have Read

1. Of the several effects of the frost that Moreton describes, which ones surprised you the most? Which one(s) can you support from your personal experience? Which ones do you think are exaggerations?

2. What is a cellar? What was the purpose of a cellar in an outport such as Greenspond in the 1850s? Was it a necessity? Why?

3. Moreton described several expedients (means) used by the people to combat the effects of the frost. How was bread prevented from freezing? Yeast? Wine? What characteristics of the people are demonstrated by such actions?

4. Despite the disagreeable aspect of the Newfoundland climate that Reverend Moreton describes, he urges young men to come to Newfoundland. For what purpose? What would be their reward?

Things To Do

1. Consider one aspect of the Newfoundland environment — its climate. If you were writing to a non-Newfoundlander to inform him/her of the most enjoyable aspect of the climate, what would you say? What would you say about the less enjoyable? (Remember to be very clear and detailed in what you say because your audience is not at all familiar with the Newfoundland climate.)

2. If Reverend Julian Moreton were to visit Greenspond today, would his description of the effects of the winter frosts be different from those contained in this selection? In what ways?

* * *

Getting Ready To Read

We often think of fog as a still or stagnant blanket of moisture. But in this poem fog is continuously moving, is not still for a second, and pervades all the different landscapes; hillsides, harbour, boglands, tree-tops, streets and buildings.

You should note that Moya Murphy gives animal or plant characteristics to the fog, but none consistently. There is a consistency, though, in the fact that each plant or animal used suggests silent, continuous, stealthy and encircling movement.

Fog is not uncommon in Newfoundland, especially on the East Coast. Considering the tragic effect that heavy fog can have for those who live by or on the sea, do you find any significance in the fifth line of stanza one and the third line of stanza four? If this causes you trouble, read the next selection by Al Pittman and then try to answer the question.

Fog Song

SWIFT as night it comes
Down the hillsides
Filling the crevasses*
Over the water
Curling 'round mastheads
Softly it glides.

Into the boglands
Tangy with salt breath
Softly at twilight
Slumb'ring in tree-tops
Circling the heath.

Through every bright street
Kissing the pavements

Damp, steamy pavements
Lifting its tendrils*
Loving the lampposts
Coiling, recoiling, stealthily, guiltily.

Writhing* and rising
Restless and quietly
Into the belfries*
Hiding the bright lights
All light extinguished
Silent and quickly.

Moya Murphy

Moya Murphy was born in St. John's and is the author of other works of poetry and several book reviews. She is a former medical technologist who is now selling real estate. The poem "Fog Song" was a prize winning entry in the 1952 F.M. O'Leary Poetry Contest.

Understanding What You Have Read

1. The poem has neither regular rhythm nor any rhyme scheme. What are its strengths as a poem?

2. List all the adverbial prepositional phrases in the order in which they appear. Now read them one after the other. What is the effect?

3. Consider what Moya Murphy meant by the last two lines. If you think there is meaning beyond the ordinary, say what it is.

Things To Do

1. List the different verbs of motion used in this poem. Add a list of adverbs which give a fuller impression of movement.

2. What living thing is brought to mind by each of the following?

    a) Curling 'round mastheads
    b) Softly it glides
    c) Slumb'ring in tree-tops
    d) Lifting its tendrils
    e) Coiling, recoiling, writhing

3. Write a short stanza of your own about fog.

4. Compare the fog in this poem with the fog in the selection by Al Pittman entitled "In the Black of Night."

* * *

Justin Hall

Getting Ready To Read

This essay by Al Pittman is unusual in form. It has the appearance on the page of a poem. If you examine it, though, you will see that it is really made up of paragraphs, that the sentences run irregularly from one line into the next, and there is not a sustained imagery. Yet, there are some elements of poetic language, such as alliteration, similies and other figurative language.

Notice that there is some new or additional action or thought in each paragraph up to the seventh. The seventh is a still picture which tries to show us the worry, tensions, fear, all the emotion of the incident, and permits us to turn toward home with the author in paragraph eight, leaving the incident unresolved.

In The Black of Night

In the black of night the news has come to us.
Two boys from Back Cove lost in the fog. They
are out on the water in an open boat and the
Lord knows there's nothing worse than fog.

The bells have brought everyone out of doors.
They huddle in groups along the fences, in the
middle of the road, and around the well. The
fog envelops them.

They do not talk in whispers but still there is a
distinct lowering of voice as though they were
afraid to speak out too loud, afraid they might
somehow muffle the boom of the invisible bells
ringing out from invisible steeples.

There is talk of bonfires along the hillside and
word now that the boats have gone out. There is

talk of a gale warning and there are names mentioned
and sympathies declared and possibilities considered.

It could be they got ashore on one of the islands.
It could be they've been picked up already. It could
even be that they might be right out there in the
cove within ring of the bells.

There is no suggestion that the worst has happened.
The bells ring as vigorously now as when they began.
Men are beginning to cut boughs for the fires and
news is passed that more boats have gone out now to
join the search.

The people remain huddled. Not one of them stands
anywhere alone. They talk in lowered voices. The
bells boom into the fog and over on the south side
there is the first flicker of flame. The bonfires
have begun.

We turn toward home to wait it out listening each
footstep of the way for a sudden silence in the night.
Waiting for that moment when word is passed uphill to
the churches, when bell ropes are released from aching
hands and left to swing giddily in their damp
chambers like nooses relieved of their dreadful
burden after a hanging.

Al Pittman

Al Pittman is one of the best known of present day Newfoundland poets. He received national recognition for his children's book **Down By Jim Long's Stage,** *but he had* *published books of poetry as early as 1966,* **The Elusive Resurrection,** *and* **Seaweeds and Rosaries** *(1970). Breakwater Books, of which he was a founder, published* **Through One More Window** *(1973),* **A Rope Against the Sun** *(1974), and* **Once When I Was Drowning** *(1978). His most recent work will be published under the title* **West Moon.** *Mr. Pittman taught English in various schools, including two years at Fogo, before joining the staff of Memorial University's English Department. He presently is on the faculty of Memorial's Wilfred Grenfell College in Corner Brook. He was born in 1940 in St. Leonard's, Placentia Bay.*

Understanding What You Have Read

1. Back Cove is in Fogo on Fogo Island. Find Fogo on a map and see if you can estimate where Back Cove would be.

2. Although not poetry, this essay does have some fine figurative language, some of it quite precise and condensed. It also makes use of effective alliteration. Find examples of figurative language and alliteration.

3. This is a "mood" piece of writing. Can you describe the mood or feeling which predominates? You should use more than one word in your description.

Things To Do

1. Explain "...invisible bells ringing out from invisible steeples.", "...listening...for a sudden silence in the night."

2. Why are sentences in the seventh paragraph so short? What purpose is served by the last paragraph?

3. Write an account of this incident as it might appear in *The Gander Beacon* or *The Lewisporte Pilot*. How is it different from Mr. Pittman's essay? Invent an appropriate ending for a newspaper account.

4. Write dialogue suggested by paragraphs four and five.

* * *

Getting Ready To Read

This essay is taken from *Wild Captives*, a book by Donald Dodds about the wild animals of the island of Newfoundland. The weasel is a common animal in most parts of the island, and is often found around farms and small communities. Many people think of the weasel as a sly, shifty thing. As a matter of fact the word "weasel" has come to mean that. In this selection, however, Mr. Dodds lets us meet Belette as an individual, and get to know something of how he lives. As you read you will be impressed by the remarkable agility and speed of this little animal, and by its ability to adapt to its surroundings and to the seasons.

Notice in this selection the author's skill in describing for us the scenes in nature as the seasons change, and the detail used in giving us an understanding of Belette's surroundings. Sight and sound are used skillfully to let us see a series of pictures, each packed with action.

This author uses a writing technique suited to his purpose. He wants us to know about the way Belette lives and dies. To do that he uses a series of highly detailed segments, each separated from the next by a period of months. We first meet Belette in winter, in the forest, at night.

Belette

The snow and the night have changed the face of the forest. Frothy white cones reach for the stars and the high, bright moon. Early that day the forest was green, but snow fell during the hours of light, stopping at dusk, and now the clear, white night is new.

In the dense fir, chickadees roost, brown caps and black caps together. Crossbills, jays, and grosbeaks sleep under the limbs and snow. In the morning, when the four-footed animals seek a sheltered rest, birds will emerge to greet the dawn and feed. If they slept till dawn was full and past, they would be safe from the predator*, but this they cannot do.

A fox calls, his beautiful, mournful cry repeated. The dog seeks a mate this February night. As if in answer, the echo sounds. Then another fox takes up the cry and there are four.

Beside a fallen birch the snow stirs. It rises slightly a few inches on one side of the quilted log, and then the magic is repeated on the other side. Suddenly the snow explodes at the base of the upturned stump. A ghost-white Belette sits up, sniffing the frosted night. The moonlight, feeling its way between the giant boughs, picks out the black-bead eyes and, against the snow cushion, the black tip of a shivering tail. Belette moves into the beam of light and faces the moon. It is very bright to his eyes but he sits motionless for several minutes.

A great white owl sails over the tree-tips near by. It swoops into the forest and perches on a crooked, snow-covered crag of birch. The owl does not hear or see the weasel, for Belette has not moved. Once covered by the bird's shadow, he waits before making the movement that might reveal his presence to the ears and eyes of the owl.

Belette sits peering straight at the moon, paws slanting downwards against his stomach. Then, in one quick movement, he is hidden by snow-cover, silent and still beneath the blanket. The owl senses no movement. No sound is audible* even to the great drum ears inside the feathered head.

One of the foxes in the moonlight comes padding through the fluff. Beneath the owl tree he stops and looks up. He moves his head about, cocking it to one side, and sits down to examine the white bird outlined against the sky. Only the head of the owl moves to watch the fox. Vulpes frisks about, tired of watching. He dives into the snow, head first, front paws digging swiftly. Small snow-clouds flurry and settle in pieces on the tail and back of the fox. Vulpe looks up from his white cave towards the owl with a snow-covered face, and burrows again.

Belette must move now. The fox is very close. There is a purpose to the game. Quickly Belette slithers through the snow to the mouse-tunnels below and at once is gone. Vulpes digs, listens, smells, and digs. There is more than one odour here. The weasel has escaped, but where the weasel is there also may be mice.

Through the fluff to the old snow crust he digs — through

the crust to the granules beneath. A movement under his paws stirs Vulpes to dig faster, leap high in the air — straight up, and down — then snap and drop the furry fluff. Vulpes holds his nose almost against the mouse, a paw resting at either side. The mouse sits up, pawing at the giant. Its teeth show and the mouth moves open and shut. Vulpes picks the mouse up gently. His lips are curled and only his incisors* grip the prey. Snapping his neck back, he throws the mouse behind him into the fluffy snow. Quickly the fox jumps up, and down again at the mouse. The squeal is heard by the owl who swerves down from his perch, sailing close to Vulpes' back. The fox turns and snaps at the passing bird, looks down, and delicately chews off the digestive tract of his meal, to leave for the first morning jay.

Belette moves through the maze of tunnels, sometimes turning in his path to back-track a distance. Everywhere is the scent of mice. He crosses tiny midden* heaps, fresh cut from rhizomes* in the loose earth beneath the winter blanket. Mouse droppings are everywhere along the track-beaten maze. At a junction he surprises a resident moving across his path. The chase is short. Belette crunches the mouse's head, his needle teeth piercing the skull, and feeds.

It is late March. When the wind blows Belette's fur, brown shows beneath the white coat. Birds are becoming active, and the weasel, lying motionless beneath alder clumps, takes more of the flying creatures than during the time of winter's deadness.

April comes and Belette is greyish in colour, the brown hair casting shadows through the lingering white. Then May arrives and Belette is brown.

He travels farther now, even though food is plentiful. It is time to breed, and he seeks the sedentary* female.

Gracilis moves out from her rock den high above the stream-bed. Over the clinging trunk roots turned quickly up by the sun and the earth, she moves over the ledge to the level ground above her. She is smaller by half than Belette. Narrower in the head and body, she is daintier, more fragile than the male, yet she disciplines her spring mate. For two weeks the weasels have shared the same den and the same food. Belette has brought small birds, beetles, and mice to the den.

The animals chatter, purr and sometimes bark. On occasion, Gracilis has found it necessary to nip Belette's ear to win her share.

Gracilis has hunted, too, but over a shorter distance and, over the days, with less success. Her needs are not as great as the male's. She is used to moving less, hunting less, eating less.

Now she moves beneath the fir stump on the ledge and out the opposite side, across the moss carpet to the big boulder, and is gone. Beneath this boulder is a den Gracilis has often known. The entrance is an opening in the moss carpet made by the near-surface root growth of a spruce tree, appearing only as a crack in the ground. Scurrying around through the fissures* created by the struggling young soil over the boulder's edge, she searches for any living thing, for food. Now, out she pops and scurries outside the tree-cover into the young grass near the old abandoned camp. Soon, there will be a host of grasshoppers here, but now she passes through the grass to the camp and the many beetles.

Belette is stirred by his mate's return. The female acts differently. She shoves her head beneath Belette's and chuckles. Belette grasps the female's neck harshly, making Gracilis bark and screech. The mating begins. It is June the tenth.

The young will not be born until the following spring, for development of the now-fertile eggs will be retarded until late the following winter. The mating over, Belette will begin to stray farther from the female's home range until his movements bring him back infrequently. But in the spring, if he survives, he may return.

Mid-July finds the many young weasels born that spring exploring the outside world for the first time. Behind their mother they scamper over and under, searching out food. Throughout the summer and fall, many are caught by birds of prey and foxes. Some are drowned attempting to cross the too-swift streams. A few die from disease.

Belette seeks out the carrion* and waste about the campgrounds this summer. He feeds on discarded meat, taking fly and beetle larvae* eagerly with the carrion. There are also plenty of grasshoppers and young birds, and Belette grows fat.

In winter, exposure to the cold above snow-cover quickly destroys a weasel careless enough to rest outside. With fat and full stomach, the fall weasel is hardier than the late winter animal.

Weasels, too,can grow lazy. The easy life about the camp prompts Belette to go on living the same way. In September, when the wind ruffles his brown fur to show the approaching white coat beneath, Belette begins a journey to the farm.

By January the white hunter has destroyed all the rats and mice from the woodshed, but there is always garbage behind the building.

Today the smell of fresh meat lures Belette to the barn. Inside hang the dripping quarters of moose. On the floor the blood puddles emit a heavy odour. Belette darts straight to the warm liquid. There is movement near him but he is fearless. It is the cat who has been given credit for Belette's hunting successes, and now Belette himself is killed. It will be unfortunate for the cat if another weasel does not now arrive to do the feline's work for him.

Back in her rock den, Gracilis lies curled, a tiny ball of deadly life, her head hidden by a stomach and tail. Within her, six minute* specks will become three male and three female weasels by spring, by the grace of many miracles.

Donald G. Dodds

Donald G. Dodds was born in the United States but has spent most of his adult life in Canada. He worked for a time as wildlife biologist and consultant for the Newfoundland Government. His observations and experiences in the field provided the material for **Wild Captives** *which was published in 1965. Since then his expertise has been employed by the United Nations, the Canadian Government, and agencies in Rome, Kenya and Zambia. Dr. Dodds has published numerous papers, short stories and scripts.*

Understanding What You Have Read

1. The author uses several words as substitutes for "snow." List them. What picture or impression is given by each? Do you think of snow that way?

2. Notice and list the choice of verbs used to describe the movements of Gracilis. What impression do you get?

3. What is your opinion of the last two paragraphs?

4. What is the meaning of the last phrase?

Things To Do

1. Find lines which give us a clear idea of the sudden movements and great speed of the weasel.

2. Think of the action, and form a mental "movie picture" suggested by "Vulpes digs, listens, smells, and digs."

3. Can you find evidence of the uncertainty of the life of the weasel? Discuss this with your teacher and classmates.

4. Compare the appearance and behaviour of Belette in September with his appearance and behavior in March.

5. What is Belette's relationship with man?

* * *

Getting Ready To Read

Many people find God in the beauties and simplicity of nature. Miss Cooper takes us into a garden and helps us see the marvels and mysteries which lie under that simplicity. Your garden is full of life of different kinds, and that life is part of your own existence and your world. You gain joy from it, and feel closer to nature as you work to make things grow.

Notice that the poem is straightforward in structure. It is free verse with a minimum of punctuation. The words used have been chosen very carefully so that the poem is packed with meaning.

To One Who Loves Her Garden

Into the dawn,
Hushed as a suspended note
Your heart and you go wrestling
With the last year's growth,
Pushing and pulling at roots
Grown out of bounds.
Pruning* a little here,
A little there —
Listening for a robin waking
In a neighbour's tree;
Small miracles of life
Make gentle impress
On your inner self
The young green things
Feel soft among your fingers
And some more vigorous with life
Push hard against your hand.
You hear God's footsteps as He comes
To cultivate with you
Your garden plot.

Georgiana Cooper

Georgianna Cooper was born in 1885 in Inglewood Forest, North West Arm, Trinity Bay. Her poem, "Lament for Inglewood," deals with the resettlement undergone by the people of this community. Her poems are found in **The Deserted Island.**

Understanding What You Have Read

1. What difference is there between "You go wrestling" and "Your heart and you go wrestling"?

2. What feelings are aroused by the middle part of the poem? What other feeling is promoted by the last three lines?

3. How does God "...cultivate with you/Your garden plot"?

Things To Do

1. Talk with your classmates about Miss Cooper's reasons for choosing early morning for her poem.

2. How many "small miracles of life" can you think of as being found in a garden?

3. Read the poem aloud. Compare it to the next poem by Gregory Power.

* * *

Getting Ready To Read

Curiosity is a natural and very obvious characteristic of children. There are so many mysteries about life, and so much that amazes us, that we can hardly ask questions fast enough. At least, that's the way it seems to a young child.

Children ask many questions which are difficult to answer satisfactorily. They sometimes cannot understand the abstract and unseen, but can grasp the concrete and visible.

In this short and pleasant poem, Gregory Power answers a child's questions about God by pointing to some of the beauties of nature.

Answering A Child

When he had timed the dark, and rolled the plains,
And drawn the master-plan of country lanes,
The Lord let down the rain one soft spring day,
Turned on the Sun and spun green miles of May.

He took a silver thread and wove a brook
Among the green — See where His finger shook
For mirth! and muted* echoes of His laughter
Ran down spring valleys ever, ever after.

Then, on the evening breeze, He played a tune;
The stars looked out — up rose the sleepy moon
That called the gnomes* and fairies out to play
By village roadways at the dusk of day.

Yes, everywhere I've seen Him, Oh! quite plain;
Some day I'll take you down a country lane,
By a farm and fold, and where the Goldenrod
Has set the wind aflame — I'll show you God.

Gregory Power

As a boy and young man Greg Power was an award-winning athlete. As a man he became an award-winning poet and short story writer, being published in Canada, the United States and Great Britain. Mr. Power was born in Dunville, Placentia Bay, and has lived most of his adult life in St. John's, serving for several years in the Liberal cabinet of Premier Smallwood. He presently lives in St. John's.

Understanding What You Have Read

1. The first two lines are introductory. What activity of God do they refer to?

2. Notice that the author is speaking in the first person, a friendly, conversational style. Can you say why this is appropriate for this poem?

3. Try to phrase in precise words what the question was which the child asked. Talk this over with your classmates.

4. How is this poem similar to the previous one by Miss Cooper?

Things To Do

1. Mr. Power has a very clear idea of what God is like and where He is. Can you refer to parts of the poem to support this statement?

2. Point to evidence that the author is sensitive to the beauties of nature.

3. If you had to pick one stanza as being your favourite, which would it be?

* * *

Peter Ball

ATTITUDES

People can be separated by more than time, distance, and physical barriers such as fences, walls and borders. They can be separated by prejudice and discrimination, dislike and distrust, jealousy and snobbery.

The writers of any country often concern themselves with the attitudes found in their people. These attitudes are often very positive: "help your neighbour," "be a friend," or "work together." But they might be very negative: "don't trust them," "we are better than they are," "take advantage of the weak." We refer to such negative attitudes often as prejudices, opinions held without taking the time to judge fairly. In this unit we explore a few of these prejudices.

Getting Ready To Read

Al Pittman in "The Border" has as his major theme social prejudice. Social prejudice exists when one group of people feel distrustful of, or superior to, another group of people. The reasons for such feelings are very difficult to discover. In reading "The Border" try to discover why the speaker hated the other people. In finding this "Why," you will arrive at a very useful truth about social prejudice.

The Border

The brook was the border.
We'd gather there on our side
above the falls
on Saturday afternoons
our pockets filled with stones
carefully selected
from the roadside gravel.

They would form up on the far side
and soon the battle would begin.
Rarely did anyone get hurt
but only because our weapons
were inaccurate at such range.

If by chance we did draw blood
we'd jump for joy
all up and down the bank
and the canyon below the falls
would resound with our victory chants.*

We never knew them by name
and never cared to.
I don't know why we fought them.
The only thing they had ever done

to us was to return stone-throw
for stone-throw.

Their only offence was
they lived across the brook.

They hated us for the same reason.

Al Pittman

Understanding What You Have Read

1. For what purpose were the stones "carefully selected?"

2. a) Who are the "they" in the poem?
   b) Why did the speaker's group throw stones at "them"?
   c) Did the speaker hate any one person of "they"? How do you know?
   d) Does the speaker know the "reason" for his hate? Was there a reason?

3. The speaker says "Rarely did anyone get hurt." Why? Would they have really hurt each other if they could? How do you know?

4. The title of the poem is "The Border." The word "border" makes you think of countries. Are the two groups in the poem like some countries we hear and read about? Explain.

Things To Do

1. Saint Stephen is a saint whose death by stoning is related in the Bible. Read the story and report it to the class.

2. Alliteration is a device used by poets to create an imitation of rhyme within a line of poetry. Alliteration is defined as the repetition of the same first sound in a line of a poem. For example, the *r*iver *r*ose repeats the "r". The *b*oys walked

*b*oldly towards the *b*ear shows alliteration of the "b". Quote examples of alliteration from "The Border."

3. If you like free verse poetry such as "The Border," you may read more of Al Pittman's poetry in his books *Once When I Was Drowning* and *Through One More Window.*

* * *

Ben Hansen

Getting Ready To Read

There was a time when male and female roles were very clear and defined. Boys played ball and killed fish, but did not knit or wash dishes. Girls played with dolls and ironed clothes, but did not whistle, or shoot birds. Boys could not aspire to become nurses, nor girls doctors. There were things which were boys' domain, and those which were girls'. Somehow, though, the boys seemed to have had the better of it. Things have changed considerably in the past few years.

This story is about the conflict created when one girl and her teacher dared to change the roles a little. It is set in a small town where the male and female roles are strongly entrenched. The teacher is from another town, River Hibbert, a little more enlightened where "girls...get to play on softball teams just like boys".

Often when a group asserts its rights and conflict begins, there is pressure from within that group to give up, to "let things alone". There is often "friendly" outside pressure too. You will find both in this story. Notice that the pressures used by the boys are psychological as well as physical, which eventually forces the teacher to take a risk to bring the matter to a conclusion. This story is more than a story about children at school.

Anne Hart opens this story with a very good description of the physical aspects of a one-room school, and the attitude towards school which students so quickly acquired in those circumstances. Pay close attention to this part and try to decide where she is being straightforward and where she is exaggerating or poking fun.

Next Week This Time

The last hour of school on Friday afternoons was for Junior Red Cross. The little kids would get out their Junior Red Cross pins and put them on and us big kids would start elbowing down the aisles to the book cupboard at the back to see who would get the interesting magazines. There was a big pile of them — brought out by a lady from town so long ago that only the oldest kids could remember it — and they were of two kinds: the *National Geographic* and the *Junior Red Cross News*. Because the boys were stronger and sat near the back they usually got the *National Geographic* first which meant they could spend the rest of Red Cross looking at African ladies wearing nothing on top while us girls had to be satisfied with the *Junior Red Cross News* which showed little African kids wearing lots of clothes and learning how to read. Apart from the magazines for the big kids and maybe the teacher reading a story to the little kids, about the only other thing that happened regularly during Red Cross was picking the two boys who would carry water the next week.

In our school the water bucket always stood on a shelf at the front of the room just behind the teacher's desk. First you'd make a paper cup out of a piece of scribbler paper (it usually took until Grade Four before you could make one that didn't leak), then you'd grab the teacher's attention from wherever it happened to be and then up you'd go to the front of the room for a drink from the water bucket.

It was kind of interesting to stand at the front of the room behind the teacher's desk and drink water. The school looked different from up there and sometimes you could get just a glimpse of an idea of what the teacher thought she was all about. I mean, from the front, looking down on those rows of kids with their heads bent over their desks and the sun coming in the windows and the blackboards and all that stuff on the walls, you might almost think, at first glance, that you were looking at one of those real city schools — like in the health books — where the kids were all so neat and all the same size. But — after that first strange moment it just became our old school again because you had to start adding in things like the coal stove and the big circle of soot it made on the ceiling above and the scarred old double desks and the kids themselves. I mean, we just didn't look like the kids in those pictures. Maybe it was because we were so many different sizes — from the little kids snuffling in the front rows over their Nan and Dan readers to the big boys hunched over their desks at the back; maybe it was because we wore so many heavy clothes all the time and never took our outdoor boots off, or maybe it was because of something that wasn't even there at all but seemed to be on the faces of those African kids in the Red Cross magazines: a look as if they liked being where they were.

Sometimes — just at the beginning — our own little kids would have that look. They'd gaze up at the teacher with big round eyes as if all that Nan and Dan stuff was really true. And enjoyable. It was funny to catch that look because you could almost remember having the same feeling yourself once and you would almost pity the poor little things knowing that look would all be rubbed off their faces long before they ever reached Grade Two. It wasn't the teachers' fault, exactly. I mean, over the years, we had some pretty nice teachers but every teacher knew and we knew and our parents knew that learning things was such hard, boring, miserable work that kids would never do it unless they were shut up all day long in a big, crowded room where they could be urged and nagged and threatened until they gave in and learned something. And it wasn't our fault, exactly, that the little kids lost that unprotected, happy look they sometimes had at first because if we hadn't teased them and taken away their lunchbox treats and taught them to hate school — just like we'd been taught — they might have grown up to be sissies or something and not able to stand up for themselves. But all that's a long way from Junior Red Cross and who would carry the water.

The water for our school came from a pump at the railway station which was about a quarter of a mile away. Long ago — maybe about the same time as the magazine lady — a Health Inspector had come around and had announced that water must be made available to the school. For a while there had even been some talk of digging a well but that had gradually died away and in the end we got a big shiny, galvanized* water bucket and permission to use the railway station pump. And from that day on — for all the boys — the most important thing that happened at school, even more important than softball, was who would get to carry the water. If you were a boy it was something you started dreaming about in Grade One even though there was not the remotest chance it could ever happen to you before at least Grade Five and only then if the teacher thought you were big enough and strong enough to pick. You dreamed about it because carrying the water meant you could get away from school for maybe an hour at a time and mostly you dreamed about it because carrying the water was something real and had absolutely nothing whatever to do with Nan and Dan and all that stuff.

So every Friday afternoon towards the end of Red Cross, when it got to be time for the teacher to pick the two boys who would go for water the next week, all the *National Geographic*s came to rest like huge butterflies folding up their yellow wings and a big hush fell all over the back rows. And that's the way it had always been until one extraordinary afternoon right out of the blue, just after the teacher had picked Ernie Chapman and Garnet Dixon to carry the water, my seatmate, Alma Niles put up her hand and said: "Why can't girls go for the water too?"

If one of those German planes, like in the war movies, had all of a sudden flown over the school and dropped a bomb we all couldn't have been more surprised! A stunned silence fell over the room and in that silence everyone looked at the teacher.

Now our teacher that year was named Miss Wilson and even though she came from River Hibbert we all liked her quite a lot. She was strict but she was never really mean like some of the teachers we'd had. Because she was young and pretty (she'd just finished Grade Eleven the year before herself. River Hibbert had fancy things like Grade Eleven) she'd had quite a rough time the first week of school with the bigger boys. But she was pretty big herself and after she'd strapped most of them up at the front of the room before our very eyes (and even the little kids could see that it really hurt) things had settled down. The boys kind of admired Miss Wilson for strapping so hard and us girls admired her because she was so pretty and wore nylon stockings and loafers all the time. But the really unusual thing about Miss Wilson — quite apart from the fact that she strapped well and wore nylons every day — was that she sometimes stopped in the middle of a lesson and looked at us as if we were real people instead of just a lot of kids who had to be pushed through to their next grades. And that was why, on that Friday afternoon when Alma Niles put up her hand and said: "Why can't girls go for the water too?" we all turned and looked at Miss Wilson first instead of just bursting out laughing at Alma right away.

And Miss Wilson, instead of saying "Whoever heard of girls going for the water?" or "Are you trying to be saucy, Alma?" like any other teacher would, said nothing at all for a moment but just looked very hard at Alma, who had gone quite white with the shock of dropping such a bombshell, and after a long moment, when she finally spoke, Miss Wilson, instead of saying "Why that's out of the question, Alma," threw a bombshell of her own.

"I'll think about that," she said — as if, you know, she would — "and I'll let you know next Friday."

The trouble started right away as soon as we got into the schoolyard because all the boys knew, from the moment Miss Wilson had spoken, that something vital of theirs was being threatened and that as long as there was the remotest chance that any girl might get to carry the water they had to do everything in their power to stop it. Like driving a tractor or playing hockey for the Toronto Maple Leafs, carrying the water was real and because it was real it belonged to them. So they went right for Alma as soon as she came out of the school and that was when another funny thing happened because the rest of us girls, instead of just standing back and watching Alma get beaten up like we usually did when the boys were after someone, rushed right in to try and help her. In the first place we all liked Alma and in the second place we all had seen, as clearly as the boys, what our carrying the water might mean: that, incredibly, we too might get to skip school for an hour at a time, that we too might get to sneak into Rowsell's store on the way back and most dizzying thought of all, that we too might get to do something real.

And because we were so intoxicated* by the whole idea and took the boys so much by surprise by standing up to them and by a lot of dodging and scratching and screeching and by threats from those of us who had brothers that we would tell at home, and above all, by all of us sticking together, we somehow managed to get Alma and ourselves out of the schoolyard and only a few bruises and torn stockings and the strap of Alma's bookbag broken, leaving the boys in possession of the schoolyard where, as we could glimpse over our shoulders as we ran down the hill, they had begun to gather together in a single ominous* knot.

And for the rest of that weekend, though of course we never talked about it in front of our parents, all we could think of, both boys and girls, was what was going to happen at school that coming week.

The first thing clearly evident by recess on Monday morning was that the boys had decided not to let us girls field at softball any more.

Softball at our school used to go like this: every Monday morning at recess two of the bigger boys — that year it was usually Ernie Chapman and Junior LeBlanc — used to pick their teams for the week. Whichever one came out on top in laddering their hands up the softball bat got to pick first and the loser second and so it went — back and forth — until all the boys who were considered good enough to be on a team had been picked. Then Ernie and Junior laddered the bat again to see which side would get up first and the losing side took to the field to be joined by the little boys who hadn't been picked and us older girls who were allowed to act as sort of permanent supplementary fielders. And for the rest of the week the teams remained locked at every recess and lunchtime, in one long softball game which had, as we discovered to our surprise several years later when the television came through, unusually complicated rules.

The way we played, for example, every single boy had to get out before the other team could come in. And any boy hitting a home run not only had the right to bat straight away again but also to bring back into the game any boy who had got out. Which led to kids who couldn't remember their six times table properly being able to announce — say, by noon on Thursday — "The score's now forty-six to thirty-nine, because, in the last inning starting Tuesday lunchtime, Junior's team was all out except for Irving Snell who hit three homers in a row off of Lorne Ripley and brought in Ira and Jim and Elton who brought in the rest except for Austin who got out for the second time on Wednesday with a fall ball one of the girls caught behind third base...."

Some days it got so exciting that at noon we couldn't wait to eat our lunches but would rush straight into the schoolyard, gobbling our sandwiches as we ran, towards that aching moment when the ball, snaking across the yellow grass or arching towards us from the marsh sky, might meet our open eager hands.

So Monday morning recess, when Ernie Chapman whirled the bat around his head, slammed it down as hard as he could on home base and announced "The first girl that goes out to field, we break her neck," was a hard blow. We clustered forlornly around the girls' entry door knowing there was nothing we could really do. "Oh Alma," mourned Minnie Halliday, biting the end of her long, brown braids, "why couldn't you just have kept your mouth shut?" It was a bad moment. If we'd tried to go out to field they'd have picked us off one by one. We couldn't even play softball on our own. None of us owned a bat and ball.

If it hadn't been for Doris Pomeroy we might have broken ranks there and then but Doris, who was in Grade Nine and had had a home permanent and sometimes wore nail polish and had even, it was rumoured, gone swimming in the Quarry all alone with Elton Lawrence, flicked a rock against the school house wall in the silence following Minnie's remark and steadied us all by saying: "Don't be foolish, Minnie. All we have to do is wait. They need us to field and, besides, they kind of like to have us out there looking at them when they get up to bat."

But it was a long, hard week. Besides not letting us field, the boys picked on us whenever they got the chance. I guess they figured if they made things bad enough for us, sooner or later we'd go to Miss Wilson and ask her to forget the whole thing. But all their picking on and bullying did was to keep us together. Whenever one of us was tripped going down the aisle or got an ink ball in her hair or got trapped in the outhouse by a bunch of boys it was as if it was happening to all of us. And looking back on that week — when there were so many bad feelings and so many new feelings in the air — it was kind of nice, too, because for the first time we girls found ourselves telling each other our troubles and even our thoughts without worrying about being laughed at. And that was something new at our school.

As for Alma, who kept getting notes thrown on her desk promising her everything from a bloody nose to having her pants pulled down, we stuck to her like burrs. But maybe Alma's hardest moment had nothing to do with bullying at all. It was when her cousin Arnold came over to see her Wednesday after school and asked her to drop the whole idea of girls going for the water.

"If they find out about it, Alma," said Arnold, "they'll probably take away the water bucket."

"Who's they?" asked Alma. She and Arnold played a lot together when they were little kids and she was used to listening to his opinions.

"Well, the Health Inspector," said Arnold, "and guys like that."

"They'll never take away that water bucket," said Alma, though she wasn't all that sure. "They don't care who carries the water as long as it gets carried."

"Alma," said Arnold, "the other guys would kill me if they ever found out I told you this but sometimes carrying the water isn't that much fun. On cold days it's real hard work. You're better off in the warm school."

Alma knew what it cost Arnold to tell her this but she stood firm. "I'm sorry, Arnold," she said, "but I'm used to cold weather. In winter I walk to school the same as you." So Arnold went away.

If Miss Wilson, as the week wore on, noticed anything unusual going on in her school she gave no sign of it. She passed out the usual punishments for ink balls, she intercepted threatening notes and tore them up unread. She looked at Alma's white face and all she asked about was the principal rivers of Europe. Nor were we surprised. Nothing in our experience had led us to believe that the grown-ups had the slightest inkling — or interest — in what really went on with kids.

Only Doris Pomeroy thought differently. "Miss Wilson looks real mad," said Doris as we trailed in thankfully from Friday morning recess.

"Mad?"

"Yeah. Like when she comes out to ring the bell and we're hanging around the entry door like scared chickens. She rings that old handbell as if she wished all those yelling boys' heads were under it. Of course, they do things differently in River Hibbert. I know for a fact that girls there get to play on softball teams just like the boys."

"On teams? Just like the boys?" But it was too much for us to take in at that moment so preoccupied were we with that afternoon's decision on the water. All that long, hard week it was as if Friday afternoon and Junior Red Cross would never come again. Now that it was almost upon us, most of us forgot, in our excitement— at least for the time being — Doris' heady remarks about softball.

So at lunchtime, just as the boys were winding up their week's game ("And real great, eh? Without the girls?" Ernie Chapman was gloating loudly from the pitcher's mound), when Miss Wilson, without her bell, leaped through our clustered huddles at the entry door and headed straight toward the softball field, she took us all completely by surprise. Crunch, crunch, crunch, went Miss Wilson's bright red loafers against the cinders and the next thing we knew she'd grabbed the bat from Irving Shell and, squinting against the sun, was twirling and lining it before our astonished eyes.

"Come on! Come on!" cried Miss Wilson impatiently to Ernie who stood transfixed before her on the pitcher's mound. "Come on! Come on!" she cried again and she banged the bat against the ground. "Come on! Come on!" cried Doris Pomeroy and we all rushed after her across the cinders.

The first ball Ernie threw was pretty wobbly and Miss Wilson hit it at an angle so that it fell sideways, a fall ball, towards George Fowler's outstretched hands. "Ah-h-h-h-h-h," we moaned from the sidelines and some of us closed our eyes so we wouldn't have to look. But George jumped too eagerly for such an easy ball and it fell right through his fingers and rolled harmlessly along the ground.

Ernie took a lot more time over his second pitch. He was getting over the first shock of finding Miss Wilson opposite him at bat and by this time he was receiving shouts of encouragement from all over the field.

"Get her! Get her!" the boys yelled recklessly at Ernie and they all fanned out behind the bases.

Ernie took aim slowly. None of us had ever seen the pirouettings* of professional pitchers but there was a certain awesome* ceremony, nevertheless, as Ernie spat savagely on the ball, glared hard at Miss Wilson, slowly swung back his big right arm and, poised for one long moment, his whole body outstretched, threw the ball as hard as he could towards home base where Miss Wilson waited, her sturdy feet braced against the cinders, her body rocking with the bat.

For a fleeting moment we had a glimpse of what life might be like in River Hibbert and then Miss Wilson hit the ball.

"Ah-h-h-h-h-h," we cried as it rose high in the air, borne by the marsh wind, and flew like a bird against the sun, across the road and out of sight, into the Ox Pasture on the other side.

"Ah-h-h-h-h-h..."

We all stared at Miss Wilson. "School's in" she announced over her shoulder, walking away.

Hitting the ball into the Ox Pasture happened maybe once a year.

That afternoon, towards the end of Red Cross, there was a big hush all over the room.

"Next week," said Miss Wilson, closing the school register, tidying her books, "next week Alma Niles and Joyce Shipley will go for the water."

She swept her hand over the top of her desk and tiny dust motes* danced in the slanting sun.

Anne Hart

Anne Hart began her writing career in 1971, and in 1974 won first prize in the Margaret Duley Short Story Contest. Her work has been published in several Canadian periodicals and magazines, including **Chatelaine** *and* **The Newfoundland Quarterly.** *One of her short stories was adapted for presentation on CBC Radio. She was born in Winnipeg, moved to Nova Scotia and then to Newfoundland. She is presently living in St. John's.*

Understanding What You Have Read

1. What is meant by "...a look as if they liked being where they were. Sometimes — just at the beginning — our own little kids would have that look."?

2. How does the author make clear the importance of being picked to go for water?

3. What indications do we have that Miss Wilson is not your ordinary, everyday teacher?

4. How did Miss Wilson's answer to Alma's question affect the boys? How did it affect the girls?

5. Why did Miss Wilson go to bat for the girls?

Things To Do

1. Do you think it was right that Miss Wilson had to show her superiority in order to have the girls gain a right to which they were entitled?

2. What could have been the outcome if Miss Wilson had struck out, or if George had caught the ball? Write a different ending for the story based on either event.

3. Compare the boy and girl situation in the story with the boy and girl situation where you live.

4. Relate this story to a minority's fight for its rights in a different setting. The native people in Labrador, or the students from a small community in a Central High School may be possibilities to use here.

5. Anne Hart lives in Newfoundland but her childhood was spent elsewhere. Any reflection on her early school days would probably be set in her own home town. There could be details in her writing which would indicate that the setting is somewhere outside Newfoundland. The surnames of the people, and the names of the towns are examples.

   (a) How many details such as these can you find to help you draw conclusions about the setting?

   (b) What similarities might make you think "this could have happened in Newfoundland"?

* * *

Getting Ready To Read

Have you been, or have you seen, a person challenged to fight who refused? Have you seen people tormented or insulted who refused to answer back? Could you understand why these people did not respond? If not, for you "The Big Fellow" will provide an explanation for such unusual but admirable actions. The poem's explanation will develop from your understanding of the two "big fellows" — a Newfoundlander and a Newfoundland dog. In reading you will come to understand that their similar opinions of their tormentors roused feelings of pity rather than abuse.

The Big Fellow

A huge six footer,
Eyes bay blue,
And as deep;
Lower jaw like a cliff,
Tongue silent,
As hard and strong as a husky.

A little man,
in a pressed suit,
Standing before him,
Had dug a name out of the past,
And flung it at him
Under cover of law.

The big fellow
Leaned over him,
Like a steel girder,
Just for a moment,
Then swung around on his heel
Without striking.

And I thought of the big Newfoundland
I saw, asleep by a rock
The day before,
That was galvanized* by a challenge,
But eyeing a cur,*
He turned,
Yawned,
Closed one eye,
Then the other,
And slept.

E.J. Pratt

Understanding What You Have Read

1. In what ways was the man like a dog?

2. What did the "little man" do when he "dug a name out of the past,/ And flung it at him/ Under cover of law"?

3. a) What is meant by "galvanized by a challenge"?

   b) What is a "cur"? Why didn't the Newfoundland dog fight with the cur?

4. If the Newfoundlander had an attitude similar to that of the Newfoundland dog, why did he not attack his attacker?

Things To Do

1. A poet, especially such a good one as E.J. Pratt, will make good use of the simile in his/ her poetry. A simile is a figure of speech that compares two different things or ideas by using "like" or "as." An example of a simile is "as quiet as death" or "a shoe like a canoe." Give examples of similes used in this poem.

2. "The Big Fellow" is an example of free verse poetry. Such poetry has no regular end rhyme and its lines are of different lengths. Could you write a short, free verse poem?

3. Read the biographical note on E.J. Pratt found at the end of "Erosion" on page 45

adamant / adj. stubborn and unyielding
Advent / n. the period before Christmas which begins four Sundays before December 25
arm / n. a long narrow stretch of water surrounded by land which leads to a harbour
astute / adj. shrewd, sly
attributed / vb. 1) credited with; 2) explained as a cause for
audible / adj. capable of being heard
awesome / adj. anything which inspires deep respect or fear
axed / vb. Newfoundland dialect for 'asked'

bangbelly- ies (plural) / n. a quick meal made from dough fried in fat back
belfries / n. towers in which bells hang
berth / n. a sailor's term for a job or position
blasty / adj. withered: a blasty bough is a dried reddish brown colour
bogey / n. small cast iron heating stove
breeks / n. same as breeches
capitalization / n. money raised to invest in a company project
capitulated / vb. submitted, stopped resisting
carrion / n. dead and decaying flesh
chants / n. words which repeat and are sung in one tone
commercial / adj. for profit
commodity / n. a product
confines / n. that which keeps within limits; restraints
constitootion / n. dialect pronunciation for constitution or the physical makeup of the individual
consumed / vb. devoured
contempt / n. disdain, the act of despising
crag / n. a steep, rugged cliff
crevasse / n. a deep crack or break especially in rock or ice
cur / n. a mongrel dog
defiant / adj. openly and boldly resisting
detractor / n. person who takes away from another's reputation
dispensary / n. a place where medicine or medical aid is given out
doughbuoys / n. dumplings generally made from flour, baking powder and water; 'doughboy' is preferred form — in general North American use
drift-ice / n. rough Arctic ice found along the coast of Newfoundland in early spring or late winter
embers / n. smoldering remains of a fire
eminence / n. a lofty or high place
entrepreneur / n. one who invests in a business enterprise
expatiated / vb. talked for a long time
fadge / vb. to make do; to thrive or succeed
fender / n. low screen in front of a fireplace
fissures / n. narrow openings or cracks

floe / n. a flat mass of floating ice
formula / n. a milk mixture for a baby
galvanized / vb. to stimulate as if by electric shock;
adj. coated over with zinc, such as an iron bucket
gnomes / n. in folklore, dwarfs who live underground and guard treasure
goaded / vb. urged on or pressured to act
guernsey / n. a heavy homespun wool handknit sweater
hangashore / n. a lazy person; angishore — a poor miserable creature (Irish derivation)
hob / n. a projecting ledge at the back or side of a fireplace
hummock / n. a rounded mound (of ice)
impel / vb. to push,to drive forward, to force
impenetrable / adj. cannot be pierced
incisors / n. any one of the front teeth in either jaw having a sharp cutting edge
inevitable / adj. bound to happen
ingenuity / n. skill in planning, inventiveness
intoxicated / vb. drunk
jostled / vb. pushed and shoved against
larvae / n. one stage of insect growth
lea / n. the protected side; lee is the preferred form
leaden / adj. sluggish, heavy, dull
leaven / n. a small piece of fermenting dough
leeward / n. situated away from the wind
littered / adj. untidy, full of litter
lurid / adj. shining with a red glow as seen through a cloud or smoke
midden / n. a rubbish heap
mimic / vb. to imitate closely; n. one who mimics
minute / adj. very small
motes / n. small particles
muted / vb.muffled or reduced sound
nectar / n. 1) any delicious drink; 2) the raw material from plants from which honey is made
obliterate / vb. to blot out, leaving no trace
ominous / adj. foretelling evil, threatening
outlandish / adj. foreign appearance or manner, strange
painter / n. rope attached to the stem of a boat
patronage / n. support or influence of a person who defends one
pell-mell / adv. in headlong confusion
peril / n. danger
philosophically / adv. sensibly composed or calm, rational
pirouetteings / n. ballet-like twirls done on the balls of the feet
poultice / n. a soft (often medicated and heated) mass spread on cloth and applied to a sore or injury
predator / n. one who lives by feeding on other animals
prestige / n. reputation, influence

pruning / vb. cutting off unwanted parts
rampikes / n. dry, knotty wood; dead trees
rhizome / n. a creeping plant stem lying at or under the surface of the soil with shoots on top and roots below
ritual / n. a set form or system of rites, religious or otherwise
rodney / n. a small, undecked, round-bottom rowboat
rounder / n. a small dried salt cod-fish which has been kept round (It is not split open to be dried flat as is done with larger cod-fish.) also 'leggie'
ruse / n. a sly trick
sarcastic / adj. speaking in a cutting or biting manner
scarp / n. a line of cliffs produced by erosion
scuppers / n. an opening in a ship's side to allow water to run off the deck
scuttle / n. a small pail for carrying coal
scuttled / vb. cut a hole in a ship in order for it to sink
sedentary / adj. very inactive, sitting a great deal of the time
sheepshank / n. a knot tied in a string or rope to take up slackness
shrapnel / n. bomb, mine or shell fragments
silhouetted / vb. outlined against a light background
slewed / vb. turned or swerved
sloughing / vb. to shed skin
soundbone / n. spinal column of cod-fish; the sound being a fatty bladder type tissue attached to the spine. Sounds may be fried and eaten.
splits / n. small pieces of wood used for kindling
tendrils / n. a slender, coiling, threadlike organ of a plant which attaches itself to a support
toutens / n. small fried cakes made from bread dough
trek / n. journey; vb. to travel slowly or laboriously
trundling / vb. rolling along
upstart / n. one who has newly or suddenly risen in importance; a newcomer in respect of rank or consequence
wallow / vb. to roll about or flounder
winnard / n. 1) side from which the wind is blowing; 2) to have an advantage over someone
writhing / vb. squirming, to twist about
zenith / n. highest point

* * *

THE CARIBOU by Joy B. Cave. First printed in the *Royal Newfoundlandland Regiment Journal*, September 1977.

CHRISTMAS and THE RITES OF SPRING by Ray Guy. Reprinted by permission of the author.

NIGHT SCHOOL. From *My Newfoundland* by A.R. Scammell (Harvest House) 1966.

PROFIT AND LOSS by Bernice Morgan. First published in *The Newfoundland Quarterly*.

TOM CODS. From *Tom Cods, Kids and Confederation* 1979 and *The Newfoundland Quarterly*.

STAGE. From *Hemlock Cove and After* by Tom Dawe.

NEWFOUNDLAND, THE WINTER FROSTS by Reverend Julien Morton. Reprinted with permission from M. Winsor.

ANSWERING A CHILD by Greg Power. First prize in F.M. O'Leary Newfoundland Poetry Contest, 1944.

NEXT WEEK THIS TIME by M.E. Anne Hart. First appeared in *Chatelaine*. Reprinted by permission of the author.

EROSION and THE BIG FELLOW by E.J. Pratt. Reprinted by permission of Mrs. E.J. Pratt

FOG SONG by Moya Murphy. From *Poems of Newfoundland 1944-1952* (F.M. O'Leary Ltd.) 1953

The publisher has made every reasonable effort to contact copyright holders of materials in this book. We would be pleased to be advised of any errors or omissions.

Special thanks to Sheila Brown for transcribing the music.

* * *

BREAKWATER *acknowledges the following photographers*

Peter Ball, pages vii, 110, 134
Jim Winter, pages 71, 72, 138
Justin Hall, pages 62, 77, 109, 120
Carol Crocker, page 86
Ben Hansen, pages viii. 138
David Wegenast / DECK'S AWASH 6

BREAKWATER *wishes to thank the* **Provincial Archives of Newfoundland and Labrador** *for the use of the photographs appearing on pages 43, 53 and 54.*

* * *